AS History
UNIT 1

Module 1: Imperial and Weimar Germany, 1866–1925

Sally Waller

Philip Allan Updates
Market Place
Deddington
Oxfordshire
OX15 0SE

tel: 01869 338652
fax: 01869 337590
e-mail: sales@philipallan.co.uk
www.philipallan.co.uk

This Guide has been written specifically to support students preparing for the AQA AS History Unit 1 examination. The content has been neither approved nor endorsed by AQA and remains the sole responsibility of the author.

Acknowledgement of copyright holders and publishers
Paper 1, Question 1 Source A, is adapted from Craig, G. (1978) *Germany 1866–1945,* Oxford University Press, by permission of Oxford University Press. Source B is from Blackburn, D. (1997) *The Long Nineteenth Century,* Harper Collins Publishers Ltd. Source C is from Waller, B. (1985) *Bismarck,* Blackwell Publishers Ltd/Polity Press. **Paper 2, Question 1** Sources A and B are adapted from Hite, J. and Hinton, C. (2000) *Weimar and Nazi Germany,* John Murray Publishers Ltd. Source C is from Alter, P. (2000) *The German Question and Europe,* Arnold Publishers.

Typeset by Magnet Harlequin, Oxford
Printed by Information Press, Eynsham, Oxford

Contents

Introduction

Aims

The AQA specification for the AS and A2 history examinations is divided into a number of different 'alternatives'. Each alternative comprises six modules or assessment units, which are generally referred to as 'units'.

This study guide is concerned with Unit 1 of Alternative G. Alternative G covers Germany from unification to reunification, 1866–1990, and Unit 1 deals with Imperial and Weimar Germany, 1866–1925.

This is likely to be the first unit that you encounter at AS, so it is important that you understand from the outset what you have to learn. This guide will provide you with the necessary information, although it should be regarded as a supplement to your textbook and other resources recommended by your teacher. If you refer to this guide throughout your course, you will find that it will help you to use your time effectively and to get the most out of your studies.

As you will be studying the development of Germany, 1866–1925 you will need to:
- examine the political, social and economic developments of the country
- assess the extent to which conditions in Germany changed or remained the same
- become familiar with differing historical interpretations of events and issues
- acquire a thorough knowledge of the period and what historians have written about it
- think for yourself, question why things happened, consider the importance of events and debate the results

This will not only prepare you for the type of questions set in the examination, but will help you to develop a greater understanding of, interest in, and enthusiasm for history.

How to use this guide

The guide is divided into two sections: Content Guidance and Questions and Answers. The Content Guidance section sets out the subject matter of the unit, breaking it down into manageable sections for study and learning. It also indicates the main themes and key concepts that you will need to cover. The Question and Answer section provides two sample papers based on the format of the AS exams. Each paper 1 question is followed by two sample answers (an A-grade and a C-grade response) with examiner comments. The paper 2 questions are followed by hints on how to construct answers and avoid common pitfalls.

Begin by working through the Content Guidance section, reading, taking notes, making charts, diagrams, tables and using other useful memory aids to ensure you have a good understanding of the period covered. You will find that certain patterns start to emerge. Make a note of these at key points along the way, so that when you have covered the whole period you are able to see the main themes and features running through it. Revise your material and add further details where appropriate. You may also need to spend some time looking at different historians' interpretations of an issue or event before moving on.

Review what you have written periodically, and test yourself using one of the sample questions in the Question and Answer section. Tackle as many sample questions as possible. By practising these questions and marking them yourself (or at least going over the marking with someone else), you will learn how to score a high grade in the examination.

Learning strategies

You can prepare yourself for this unit in various ways.

Reading and taking notes

- You will need a good set of notes. These must be clearly laid out under the headings suggested in the Content Guidance section, and should record events and issues with reference to *why* they happened, *what* happened, and *with what result*.
- Consult several books for each subsection, as authors can differ in their coverage and interpretation of events. If you find the language or style difficult, try one of the books specifically written for AS. Alternatively, ask a teacher to explain it to you. *Never* make notes on something you do not understand.
- Summarise the main points of each paragraph or section of the book you are looking at, but do not make detailed notes straight away. Look at a second book (or more) until you understand the topic and are familiar with any differing viewpoints. When you have reached this stage, begin to make more permanent notes.
- Take information from different books, rearranging the material under headings to suit your purposes. You may want to take a quotation from a book, but do not simply copy large chunks of material. Notes should be your own. Using your own words will ensure that you understand what you have read and will help you to learn more effectively.
- You will find other points to add to your notes in the course of class discussions, later reading and revision, so leave space for these. Keeping your notes in a ring binder prevents them from getting muddled up; you can always add extra sheets where necessary.

Familiarity with source material

In the examination, question 1 will be based on source extracts, so familiarise yourself with different views of issues and events by summarising these in your notes and adding supporting quotations from books. Pictorial material or cartoons which convey a relevant message may be useful. Some knowledge of why interpretations differ is also worth recording. Consider which view you find the most convincing and why. By questioning yourself, you will become more familiar with the period you are studying.

Understanding terms and concepts

If you come across any words or concepts that you do not understand, look them up in a dictionary or history textbook. It is helpful to keep a glossary of such words or terms in your file; the glossary at the end of this introductory section might be a starting-point for this. If you cannot work out the meaning of a word or are unsure that you understand it properly, ask your teacher.

Practising examination questions and answers

As you reach the end of each Content Guidance section, test yourself with a practice examination question. Examples of these are given in the Question and Answer section of this guide and your teacher may supply further examples. Your first attempts may involve looking back at your notes, but you should try to do some questions without looking anything up. If you time yourself while doing this, you will gain examination practice and this will enable you to find out your own strengths and weaknesses. Sample answers with mark allocations are also given in the Question and Answer section, so you can mark your own paper, or better still, swop with a friend who has also tried the same question and mark each others' papers. This will show you what is required to gain good marks in the examination.

Revision planning

If you have worked sensibly through the material and themes, revision should not be a problem. You will have a good set of well-organised notes and you will already be aware of the important themes of the period. You will also have practised some examination questions, both with and without the aid of your notes.

Revision should never consist of simply reading through your notes. Make a realistic timetable so that you know exactly how much time you are able to devote to your revision of Unit 1. Try using some of the following ideas:

- Rewrite your notes, focusing on the important items to remember.
- Reorganise your material to make it more meaningful.
- Try to master your work in short sections.
- Start each revision session with a review of the previous session.
- Check anything you do not understand.
- Talk about what you have learnt with someone else.
- Try to link new material with what you have already learnt.
- Make charts, diagrams, chronological lists and other learning aids (examples of these can be found in the Content Guidance section).
- Attempt some examination questions.
- Write outlines/detailed plans for some possible essays (look at the plans in the Question and Answer section for examples of how to go about this).

Examination skills

Your examination is a written test and you will need to be able to write in a clear and effective manner. The best way to improve written communication skills is to practise answering both short-answer questions and those demanding extended writing, as given in the Question and Answer section.

You have to answer two questions in the examination. Question 1 is compulsory and you will choose either question 2 or question 3. All questions are divided into three parts:

- Part (a) carries 3 marks and therefore requires a short answer.
- Part (b) carries 7 marks and requires a short answer, although longer than (a).
- Part (c) carries 15 marks and requires a piece of extended writing.

Part (a): 3-mark questions

The most important skill you will need for your examination is knowing how to select the relevant material to answer a question. This is particularly important for questions that carry only 3 marks. Practise writing brief answers of two or three sentences, which deliver the relevant information clearly and concisely. Marks are not awarded for the amount you write, but for the quality of your answer.

- Question 1(a) will ask you to *explain briefly* the importance or significance of something in the given source material.
- Questions 2(a) and 3(a) will ask *what is (or was) meant by* a term or phrase given in some stimulus material.

These questions do not simply require dictionary definitions: make it clear that you understand the given reference and its *historical context*.

Part (b): 7-mark questions

There is a slight difference between question 1(b) and questions 2(b) and 3(b), but both kinds of question require answers of no more than one or two paragraphs.

- Question 1(b) will ask you to compare sources. You may be asked to *explain how* or *in what ways* one source supports or challenges another. Your answer needs to be comparative, which means that points need to be extracted and compared across the sources. Remember that it is not usually enough to describe the differences between what the sources say. A good answer will also explain the differences.
- Questions 2(b) and 3(b) will use similar words, such as *explain why*, to invite you to look at the development of an issue or event. You should not only relate *what* happened, but also *why* it happened.

Part (c): 15-mark questions

Questions 1(c), 2(c) and 3(c) will ask you to explain an event or issue with command words such as *why* or *in what ways*. Alternatively, you may be given a quotation which asks you to '*explain why you agree or disagree with this statement*'.

These answers require a piece of extended writing. Identify the key words of the questions and write a short essay plan based on these before you begin. You should give a brief introduction (two or three sentences are sufficient) followed by clear paragraphs outlining the relevant historical events and issues. A long narrative of events by itself will not score highly; nor will opinions with no evidence to back them up. You need to combine the two and present a case that is supported by precise evidence.

Provide a conclusion at the end of your answer which links and balances the various factors you have mentioned, summarises your thoughts and makes your judgement clear. Do not be tempted to skip the conclusion. Leave the examiner in no doubt as to your views.

Glossary of common pitfalls

The following glossary may help you to avoid some of the more common pitfalls encountered by candidates studying this period of history. Do personalise it by adding words and concepts that have caused you problems.

Common spelling errors: although you are not directly penalised for these, it creates a poor impression and suggests you have done little reading if you get them wrong. Words subject to frequent errors include Bismarck, Reich, Kaiser, Hindenburg, Weimar and Stresemann.

Political terms: terms such as conservative, liberal etc. should have lower case letters when referring to the ideas, and capital letters when referring to actual political parties. Whenever possible, use precise names for political parties. SDP or SPD is acceptable for 'Social Democratic Party', but you should write 'National Liberal Party' in full, not Nat Libs in an answer.

The word 'Reich': take care with the word 'Reich', which literally means 'empire'. The empire created by Bismarck in 1871 is called the Second Reich (capital letters) to distinguish it from the First Reich or Holy Roman Empire founded by Charlemagne. The Second Reich lasted from 1871 to 1918 and is sometimes known as the *Kaiserreich*. It should not be confused with Hitler's Third Reich, from 1933 to 1945.

The Weimar Republic: the Weimar Republic was the name of the government in Germany from 9 November 1918 to 30 January 1933 and was so called because it met in Weimar, as Berlin was too dangerous in 1919. It is incorrect to say, 'Weimar did this or that' or, worse still, 'the Weimar...' (using Weimar as a noun) as in 'the Weimar was set up in 1918'. It was the politicians who took the decisions. A president (not the chancellor) headed the Weimar Republic. He was elected and was the head of state. There were two presidents in the Weimar Republic: Friedrich Ebert (1919–25) and Paul von Hindenburg (1925–34). There were, however, many chancellors. Do not confuse the two.

Content Guidance

The material required in Unit 1 can be divided into three main content areas plus an introductory area. A summary of these is given below.

This Content Guidance section provides a detailed explanation of exactly what you need to know and the key terms and themes you should be familiar with. Make sure that you have understood each subsection before moving on to the next one.

Germany up to 1866

Although the purpose of this unit is to look at developments in German history *after* 1866, you will need to know a little about the history of Germany before 1866 in order to make sense of what follows.

Germany, 1866–90

This section covers the period from the final unification of Germany and the establishment of the German empire in 1871 to the fall of the first chancellor of that empire, and the man who had done so much to create it, Otto von Bismarck.

Germany, 1890–1914

This is the period between the dismissal of Bismarck and the outbreak of the First World War. During this time Kaiser Wilhelm II exercised a strong influence on the direction of German policy, while economic growth was also a key factor affecting Germany's development.

Germany, 1914–25

This section spans the period from the outbreak of the First World War to the time of Stresemann's leadership from 1923 to 1925. The First World War brought about the collapse of the system of government that had been established in Germany. The Kaiser abdicated in 1918 and a republic (under a president) replaced the empire. This created many political and economic difficulties, but the country eventually became more stable by 1925.

Germany up to 1866

You should begin by familiarising yourself with the major developments in German history since 1815. Although you should not spend too long on this background material, you should be aware of:

- the division of Germany into separate states after 1815
- the growing desire for greater unity in Germany, particularly among German liberals
- the economic development of the German states
- the strength of Prussia and the ambitions of Otto von Bismarck, its Minister-President from 1862

The *key theme* you need to be aware of here is the position and influence of the **liberals**.

The liberals

It is important that you understand the part of the liberals in the unification process so that you can follow their influence in the later years. German liberals, like those elsewhere in Europe, believed in individual freedom so that men could meet, write and speak as they chose. They also felt that the people should have an influence on the way their country was governed. They wanted constitutions to provide a system of government whereby the wealthier and educated members of the population could vote for an elected parliament.

Many of these desires had been met, at least in part, by the constitutions set up in many of the German states in the years after 1815, but liberalism came to be associated with something more — a desire for national unity. Liberals felt that the unification of Germany was the logical outcome of their moves to break the control of the rulers of the individual states. It also offered the opportunity for greater freedom of trade and economic development, which was another liberal priority. Although the liberals did not approve of Bismarck's methods and the unification of Germany through war, they did approve of the outcome — a single German state. However, their ideas of how that state should be ruled and how it should develop were to clash increasingly with those of its new masters. Much of the history of this period is concerned with the clash between liberal and traditional conservative views.

Germany, 1866–90

For this period you need to know the following:

- The steps by which Germany finally achieved political unification (1866–71). This includes Bismarck's victory against Austria, the creation of the North German Confederation in 1866 and the war against France in 1870, which led to the creation of the new empire in January 1871 (see chart below).
- The way in which the new German empire was governed. You will need details of the constitution of the new empire, the place of the Reichstag and Bundesrat and the role of the Kaiser and the Chancellor (see diagram on p. 14).
- Bismarck's domestic policies and his achievements and failures as Chancellor. This is a big topic and it is helpful to divide it into sections. The first section would include Bismarck's Kulturkampf and May Laws (a campaign against the Catholics). The changes of 1878–79 and the decision to abandon free trade in favour of protective tariffs would lead to the second section — the campaign against the socialists, including Bismarck's own attempt to introduce socialist policies.
- The various influences which affected policies and developments. The part played by political groups such as the conservatives, liberals, Catholics and socialists, and influential groups in society such as the army and the élites (powerful people in industry and agriculture).
- The strengths and weaknesses of Germany at the time of Bismarck's fall from power. This would include some detail on the development of Germany in these years; in particular the moves towards greater unification, and the growth of trade and industry. The reason for Bismarck's dismissal and the political state of Germany at this point also need consideration (see table on p. 16).

The political unification of Germany, 1866–71

As well as making detailed notes, you may find it helpful to construct time charts to accompany some of the bullet points listed above. The chart below, based on the first point — the final steps to unification — may give you some ideas.

War with Denmark   War with Austria

1864	1865	1866 North German Confederation	1867
Prussia and Austria fight Denmark over Schleswig-Holstein.	*August* Convention of Gastein. *October* Meeting with Napoleon III at Biarritz.	Seven Weeks War. Austrian defeat at Königgratz (Sadowa). Treaty of Prague. Secret treaty with southern states.	Customs union between North German Confederacy and southern states.

There are also *key terms* and *themes* that you need to understand in order to appreciate this material.

The influence of political groups

Kulturkampf/Catholics/Centre Party

Germany was predominantly a Protestant country but there was, nevertheless, a large Catholic minority who looked to the Pope in Italy as the head of the Church. It was to protect their interests that the Zentrum, or Centre Party, was founded in 1870. This party also attracted those hostile to Bismarck and was strong in Bavaria and the Rhineland.

Bismarck was alarmed by the success of the Centre Party in 1871, when it won 61 seats in the Reichstag elections. He feared that its first loyalty might be to the Pope and he disliked its support of the nationalist Catholic Poles of the eastern provinces. When his laws against the Catholic Church in 1872 and 1873 only increased the strength of the Centre Party, he launched into the Kulturkampf, or the 'struggle for civilisation'. It failed to reduce Catholic support and by 1874 the Centre Party had 91 seats in the Reichstag; by 1878 it had 94. The campaign was subsequently abandoned, but the Centre Party remained an important political force.

Socialists

Socialism had grown in Europe with the growth of industry in the nineteenth century and it challenged traditional methods of government and ways of living and working. Inspired by Karl Marx (who wrote *Das Kapital* in 1867), two German workers' parties joined in 1875 to create the new Social Democratic Party. The German socialists believed that the workers should take over the ownership of important industries in order to give the workers a fair share of the profits; they also wanted a German republic, with rule by 'the people' rather than the Kaiser. However, they knew their aims were unrealistic and in the short term were prepared to campaign through the Reichstag. They fought in the elections of 1877 and won 12 seats. Although this was only a small number, Bismarck feared their growth and issued an anti-socialist law in 1878. His attempt to crush the socialists, rather like his earlier onslaught on the

1868	1869	1870	
Customs parliament established.	Spanish throne vacant. Offered to Leopold of Hohenzollern.	French object. Wilhelm I's Ems telegram made to appear insulting. War with France. Prussian victory at Sedan. Napoleon III deposed. Paris beseiged.	War with France / 1871 *January* Paris forced to surrender. 18 June Wilhelm I proclaimed German Emperor at Versailles. Second Reich established.

Catholics, did not work, and conversely led to an increase in their numbers and strength. By 1884 they had 24 seats; by 1890 they had 35.

Conservatives

Conservatives dislike change and favour strong government. In Germany, the land-owning nobility (or 'Junkers', as they were called in Prussia) maintained a consider-able conservative influence. The new constitution of Germany and the interests of its Chancellor, Bismarck, himself a Prussian landowner, generally ensured conservative success. Bismark increasingly relied on the Conservatives in his later years. The newly powerful industrialists, some of whom were as wealthy as the large landowners, joined the 'traditional' conservatives in the late 1870s, making a formidable force. The German Conservatives and the *Reichspartei* (another conservative party) represented them in the Reichstag and in 1878 they increased their seats from 78 to 116.

The Imperial Constitution, 1871

Clearly, the interaction between the various political parties is an important theme in this period, but you must remember that it was in the Reichstag that these rivalries were played out, because this was the *elected* part of the constitution. Diagrams, such as the following one of the Imperial Constitution of 1871, can be very helpful in showing the structure of government clearly. Diagrams also provide a useful memory aid for revision purposes.

Kaiser

German emperor and king of Prussia (hereditary). Made all government appointments, including the chancellor. Could summon/dissolve Reichstag. Supreme warlord. Commanded army and navy — could declare war and peace.

Chancellor and government ministers

Formulated government policy to present to Bundesrat. Chancellor tried to ensure support for legislation. Could advise Kaiser to dissolve Reichstag.

Bundesrat

Met under chairmanship of Kaiser or chancellor. Legislation began here.

Jointly made laws

Reichstag

Considered legislation presented by Bundesrat. Had the right to approve budget annually — the only decision which could not be overturned by the Bundesrat.

Chosen by the governments of the 26 states. Prussia had 17 representatives. Fourteen votes needed for a veto.

Elected by constituencies every 5 years by men over 25.

Elites and the army

Another theme which features in this section, and which runs throughout the whole period you will study, is that of the influence of **the élites and the army**. Ensure that you understand these terms in relation to developments between 1866 and 1890, and when you have studied the later Content Guidance sections look at this theme again.

The élites of Germany were those with sufficient wealth, status, connections and power to influence policy and place pressure on the government to protect their interests. The élites included the powerful Junkers and industrialists and the institutions they dominated such as the army and diplomatic corps. The army was a particularly powerful institution in Germany. Prussia had a strong military tradition and it was through the army and war that Germany had been united. Consequently, the military officers, recruited from the Prussian Junker class, expected to have influence over policies. They were natural conservatives, supported anti-socialist measures and had a strong belief in Germany's national greatness.

In time these élites were strengthened by the creation of other pressure groups such as the Pan-German League (1891–94), which pressed for a more energetic foreign policy; the Agrarian League (1893), which campaigned on behalf of German farmers; and the Colonial League (1882), which tried to sway public opinion in favour of overseas expansion. These élites were to have a very important part to play and a lot to answer for in the development of German policy under Kaiser Wilhelm II.

Strengths and weaknesses of Germany in 1890

In order to assess the strengths and weaknesses of Germany in 1890, you will need to consider the growth of the German economy. This is another key theme that you will need to return to after studying the later Content Guidance sections. Ensure that you understand that German industry expanded rapidly, particularly from the 1880s, and that the abandonment of free trade was both a symptom and a cause of this.

Free trade

Free trade grew from the liberal belief in freedom of enterprise. Liberals believed that laws should not restrict trade and business and that freedom allowed for healthy competition. Therefore they opposed tariffs or customs duties, and argued that goods should pass freely between seller and purchaser. Until 1878, when the National Liberal Party was powerful in Germany, free trade was practised and very low customs duties were charged on goods coming into Germany. This had worked well when the competitors were roughly equal, but during the 1870s Prussian landowners, such as Bismarck, were increasingly challenged by the large, cheap consignments of grain that arrived in steamships from the USA. Furthermore, the German factory owners found it increasingly hard to compete with the established industrialists of Great Britain, who produced goods in larger quantities and were therefore able to sell more cheaply.

The abandonment of free trade after 1878 marked the decline in the influence of the liberals.

The following provides you with a skeleton outline of Germany's strengths and weaknesses in 1890. Refer back to your notes and see if you can expand it to make a useful revision guide.

Strengths	Weaknesses
Germany was united. Written constitution. Elected Reichstag.	Prussian dominance. Reichstag had little real power. Chancellor dependent on Kaiser.
Government stability — opponents defeated. Kulturkampf against Catholic Centre Party. End of free trade weakened liberals. Anti-socialist legislation — socialist activity curbed.	Parliamentary government stunted by Bismarck's methods. Centre Party not defeated, but resentful. Socialists feeling bitter, and support growing.
Economically successful. Growth in heavy industry and new chemical/electrical industries. Growing population.	Urbanisation creating tensions — problems of housing and working conditions. Workers attracted to socialism — potential threat from Socialist Party in the future.
Militarily powerful. Large army — 500,000. Respected abroad.	Pressure for world policies — Colonial League (1882) and colonial expansion which encouraged ambition and was a drain on finance.
Established for 20 years — future looked bright.	New Kaiser unstable, irresponsible and mainly interested in military matters.

Germany, 1890–1914

The main areas to examine are as follows:

- Economic and social change and their effects, in particular the growth of socialism. The reasons for, and results of, the growth of German industry and the new tensions in society as the urban working class grew.
- Politics and the contribution of the various chancellors. The policies, successes and failures of Caprivi (1890–94), Hohenlohe (1894–1900), Bülow (Foreign Minister from 1897 and Chancellor 1900–09) and Bethmann-Hollweg (1909–17).
- Specific influences affecting political developments, in particular:
  (a) Wilhelm II — his personality, interests and ambitions, especially his militarism, his interest in the navy and his concern for *Weltpolitik* and foreign affairs. Particular interventions by the Kaiser, such as the Kruger telegram, the *Daily Telegraph* interview and the Zabern Affair, need consideration.
  (b) The army — the part played by the military in German society.
  (c) The élites — both the powerful industrialists and the landowners — mainly the Junkers who owned huge estates in Prussia. Note also the effect of pressure groups such as the Agrarian League, the Pan-German League and the Colonial League.
- Foreign policy as an influence on domestic affairs. This became particularly important under Bülow with the Hottentot election (1907), the reaction to the Anglo–Russian Entente (1907), the *Daily Telegraph* affair (1908), the Moroccan crises (1905 and 1911), the Balkan crises (1908 and 1912–13), and the events of summer 1914.
- The condition of Germany before the outbreak of war; in particular the state of German politics, society and the economy.

Two *key themes* underlying the whole of this period are **economic and social change** and **the growth of socialism**.

Economic and social change

Industrial expansion

From the 1880s German industry expanded rapidly. This was largely based on an abundant supply of raw materials, particularly in Alsace-Lorraine and the Ruhr. A rapidly growing population provided the market and workers, while social conditions in Germany helped produce a number of well-educated and forward-thinking factory owners, bankers, inventors and skilled operators to sustain the growth. Traditional heavy industries grew rapidly. The figures speak for themselves. Coal and lignite output increased from 89.1 million tons in 1890 to 279 million tons in 1913, pig iron output grew from 4.66 million to 14.79 million tons between 1890 and 1910, and steel from 3.16 million to 13.15 million tons in the same period. Germany's railways and merchant navy grew spectacularly in response to changing demands.

Germany was also particularly successful at developing newer industrial products such as electrical goods, cars and chemicals. It became a world leader in electrical engineering with successful companies such as Siemens, AEG and Daimler. Germany was fast becoming a competitor to Great Britain, and by 1913 its share of world trade had almost reached that of its rival.

Economic change brought social change. By 1910 more Germans were working in industry than in agriculture, and towns and cities were growing fast. Working and living conditions could be harsh, but in general living standards rose as the country grew wealthier. However, those who were dependent on agriculture did not share this prosperity. The competition of imported grain from the USA, carried in steamships across the Atlantic, forced a drop in grain prices, which particularly hit the Junker farmers of East Prussia.

The growth of socialism

The growth of the industrial working class led to a growth in support for the Socialist Party. Bismarck's persecution had not succeeded, and one of the causes of his dismissal had been Kaiser Wilhelm II's belief that he could deal more successfully with the workers himself. His first chancellor, Caprivi, followed a 'new course', permitting the Social Democratic Party to meet openly again and passing some reforming legislation. However, the result was not what the Kaiser had anticipated and he was horrified when the Social Democrats won more votes than any other party in the Reichstag elections of 1893. The Erfurt Programme of 1891 had alarmed not only the Kaiser, but also the factory owners, landowners and officials who feared a loss of power. Proposals such as 'the abolition of class rule' and 'the making of new laws to be controlled by the people' made them fearful that any concessions to socialism could be the first steps towards revolution.

In practice, there were still plenty of moderates or 'revisionists' within the SDP who were prepared to work within the constitution, but after 1894 the Kaiser adopted an anti-socialist stance.

There was some reforming legislation, particularly in the time of Bülow's chancellorship, but the Erfurt Programme gave the élites all the ammunition they needed to oppose the socialists. Whether or not they genuinely believed that making concessions to the Social Democrats would lead to revolution, they pretended to do so. They did not want to give up their power and contribute towards better living and working conditions, and their attitude helped to create a split in German society under a Kaiser who followed no consistent policy.

The chart opposite maps the growth of socialism up to 1912.

1863
General Workers' Association founded by Ferdinand Lassalle.

1864
Social Democratic Workers' Party founded by William Liebknecht and August Bebel.

1875
Foundation of Social Democratic Party committed to social and political reform.

1891
Erfurt Programme. SDP adopted official Marxist line — committed to overthrow of capitalism.

1900
Revisionist motion to work through Parliament defeated, but many still campaigned for and in the Reichstag.

Left wing under Karl Liebknecht and Rosa Luxemburg maintained Marxist beliefs.

Majority worked through Reichstag to block unpopular legislation.

1877 12 seats	**1884** 24 seats	**1887** 11 seats	**1890** 35 seats	**1893** 44 seats	**1898** 56 seats	**1903** 81 seats	**1907** 43 seats

1912
110 seats
Largest party in Reichstag.

1878 Anti-Socialist Law. This banned any group or meeting aimed at spread of socialist ideas.
1887 Bismarck's Anti-Socialist Kartell (Conservatives and National Liberals).
1883–89 Attempt to win workers' support through 'state socialism'.

1890–94 Anti-Socialist Laws relaxed under Caprivi.
1894–99 Government attempts at anti-socialist legislation largely unsuccessful.
1897+ *Sammlungspolitik* in an attempt to gather élites to oppose SDP.

Kaiser Wilhelm II

Another key area for study is **Kaiser Wilhelm II**. Try to read some biographical accounts of the Kaiser, or at least dip into the various descriptions of his personality presented in your books. They make fascinating reading.

Much has been written about his contradictory moods, his personal sensitivity (often attributed to the partial paralysis he suffered at birth and his tense relationship with his parents), his love of military company, and his failure to understand his subjects or the workings of his country's constitution. A question which pervades this period is the extent to which the Kaiser was responsible for the problems of Germany and its failure to develop into a modern democracy.

The constitution of 1871 gave the Kaiser enormous powers, as Bismarck found to his cost when he was dismissed in 1890. It is often remarked that those powers were tested to their full by Kaiser Wilhelm II, and used in a way that had not been envisaged in 1871. The new Emperor, who boasted that he had never read the German constitution, was determined to play an active role in government. He was full of energy. He believed his position was the gift of God and he spent much of his reign travelling around and giving his opinions on everything and anything — regardless of whether he knew much about it or not. In reality, he had little understanding of the forces then shaping Germany, in particular the growth of industry, the position of the working class, urbanisation and socialism.

In government he changed from one policy to another, dismissing his chancellors at will and so eroding their power. The Reichstag, although not totally ineffectual, was largely ignored, and as civil government was weakened he allowed the army to play an increasingly dominant role in the formulation of policy. His personal pronouncements (as in the *Daily Telegraph* interview), his prejudices (as in the Zabern affair), and his ambitions (revealed in his *Weltpolitik*) certainly influenced the development of the German state. But it must also be remembered that German society itself was divided and full of tensions, and that the Kaiser was under enormous pressure to protect vested interests.

Changes in Germany, 1890–1914

Before leaving this section, spend a little time reflecting on **the extent to which Germany had changed between 1890 and 1914**. You could start with a diagram such as the one of Germany in 1914, below.

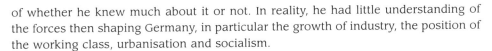

Kaiser Wilhelm II
An unstable and irresponsible leader whose interventions in government could cause trouble, e.g. the 1908 *Daily Telegraph* incident. Favoured the military and *Weltpolitik* and was determined to show his, and Germany's, power.

Political structure
Despite a constitution and elected Reichstag, power remained in the hands of the Prussian Kaiser, Chancellor and élites. From 1912 the Reichstag was dominated by socialists demanding more power.

Economy
A rapidly developing economy meant Germany was challenging Britain as a world leader. Both old and new industries were expanding. There was an 8% growth rate p.a. between 1890 and 1914.

Germany in 1914

Nationalism
Social Darwinism, which taught that strong states prosper and weak ones die, was gaining credence in all classes. This supported an aggressive foreign policy and imperial expansion — *Weltpolitik*.

Elites
The conservative élites had helped create the Reich and were hostile to reform. Old élites (Junkers) and newer élites (big businessmen) and élite pressure groups dominated society and government.

Army
A powerful élite group which basked in a glorious reputation (wars of unification) and seemed above civilian law (Zabern, 1913). The rapid growth of the navy also encouraged military pretentions. The army pressed for war in 1914, when the majority of Germans (including the SDP) rallied in support.

Socialism
This grew rapidly in response to the support of the expanding industrial and urban working class. The SDP, created in 1875, grew to the largest party in the Reichstag by 1912. The left wing followed a Marxist line, but most were prepared to work within the constitution.

You could make a similar diagram of Germany in 1890 and then draw up a table to compare the differences, as shown below.

	Germany in 1890	Germany in 1914	Reason for change/ similarity
Political structure			
Rulers			
Economy			
Elites			
Socialism			
Army			
Nationalism			

Tables to show the changes in the fortunes of the various political parties can also be useful for revision. Keep them simple, and try to learn a few of the figures to quote in your examination.

Main political parties	1884	1898	1912
Conservatives	78	56	43
Progressives (Liberals)	67	41	42
SDP	24	56	110

Seats won by main political parties between 1884 and 1912

AS History

Germany, 1914–25

You will need to know the following:

- The impact of the First World War on Germany — in particular the political breakdown and the formation of the new republic.
- The reasons for, and the events and effect of, the 'German revolution' of 1918–19. (You should, in particular, be familiar with the impact of the Versailles agreement.)
- The political and economic difficulties of the Weimar government up to 1923, the policies of the Weimar politicians, in particular Ebert and Stresemann, and the extent to which these difficulties were overcome by 1925.
- The position of Germany in 1925 — its strengths and weaknesses.

Outbreak of war. Schlieffen Plan failed to bring quick victory. First Battle of Marne and Ypres. Russian defeats in East Prussia.	**1914**	Patriotic support from all parties including SDP. Chancellor Bethmann-Hollweg disliked by right wing for failure to reform at home. Regarded as too cautious by Falkenhayn, who replaced Moltke as Chief of General Staff. Kaiser detached.
Most German colonies captured. Second Battle of Ypres — stalemate in West. German forces captured Warsaw.	**1915**	Bethmann-Hollweg quarrelled with Reichstag over the use of submarine warfare, to which he was opposed, and with the Kaiser over the need to replace Falkenhayn.
Battle of Verdun failed to break deadlock. Battle of Jutland — indecisive. Brusilov offensive on Eastern Front, Allied offensive on Somme.	**1916**	Paul von Hindenburg (who had led troops in East) put in overall command of German forces, replacing Falkenhayn with Erich von Ludendorff in control of war policy. Reichstag passed motion that the Chancellor should be guided by Supreme Command.
Unrestricted submarine warfare. USA declared war on Germany. Third Battle of Ypres (Passchendaele) — still deadlock. Russian withdrawal after Bolshevik Revolution.	**1917**	Kaiser, military and Reichstag won submarine issue. Radicals opposed to war formed USPD (Independent Socialist Party). Reichstag voted for peace. Under pressure from military, Bethmann-Hollweg forced to resign. Fatherland Party founded — wanted peace *with* land.
Treaty of Brest–Litovsk. German Spring Offensive — apparent success followed by losses in second Battle of Marne and retreat to Hindenburg Line. Germany signed armistice.	**1918**	Strikes, political speculation, food shortages. Military repression at home — harsh peace on Russia. Ludendorff rejected all arguments for peace until failure of offensive in September. Prince Max became Chancellor (October) of a civilian government and tried to introduce reforms. Armistice negotiations. Republic proclaimed (November). Kaiser abdicated.

Economic
Agricultural production fell but industry made huge profits. Mark lost 75% of value and war financed by loans and printing money (only 16% of cost came from taxation). Inflation occurred. Approximate cost of war £8,394m.

Effects

Social
Two million killed, 6.3 million wounded. Deaths also from starvation, cold and 'flu epidemic of 1918. Inflation, rationing — fall in standards of living, e.g. meat consump-tion 12 % of prewar level. Strikes and resentment of industrial profits by workers. Junkers suffered, big businessmen flourished, middle classes disillusioned.

Political
The new civilian government, based on Reichstag support (including liberals and socialists), answered the problems of the German constitution, but it came too late to save the Kaiser or the élites: by November 1918 Germany was a republic, under the socialist Ebert. 'Revolution' broke out as naval mutinies and workers' 'soviets' challenged authority.

The political break-down of Germany during the First World War

The political breakdown of Germany during the First World War

The **political breakdown** of Germany during the First World War can sometimes prove confusing. This is an occasion when a chronological diagram can be helpful. Try to do more than simply list events. In the diagram on p. 22 the course of the war is charted on the left-hand side, and the resulting changes in government on the right. It also shows the effects of war, economically, politically and socially.

The 'German revolution'

The significance and effect of the **'German revolution'** is a *key theme* in this section. Modern historians have questioned how close Germany came to revolution in these years and have criticised the way in which the 'revolution' was handled. To understand this theme, first list the basic sequence of events:

October 1918 — Prince Max, supported by the Reichstag including the liberals and the socialists, takes control of government. Begins armistice negotiations.
Naval mutinies at Wilhelmshaven and Kiel. Soviet-style councils set up in major cities and ports of northern Germany.
Eisner proclaims a Bavarian Democratic and Socialist Republic in Munich.
Riots in the Ruhr and throughout Germany.

November 1918 — The Kaiser abdicates. Prince Max hands the chancellorship to the socialist leader, Friedrich Ebert.
Ebert makes an agreement with General Groener to gain the support of the army to put down unrest.
Armistice signed.

January 1919 — Spartacist revolt crushed — followed by suppression of further strikes and uprisings.

February 1919 — National Assembly in Weimar begins work on a new constitution.

April 1919 — Revolutionary regime in Munich destroyed by the *Freikorps*.

Now try to ask yourself how the politicians felt at the time. Is it possible to explain why Ebert reacted as he did? This is often a useful way of developing an insight into a controversial historical topic.

Why did the revolutionary events seem so frightening?

In 1918 the Russian Revolution was only a year old. Memories of the overthrow of authority were still fresh in the minds of those who were trying to restore order to Germany after the calamitous events of war. For the first time the moderate socialists were being given an opportunity to influence the future of Germany. They did not want to throw away their chance in concessions to the extreme left wing.

Nevertheless, it is understandable that the parallels with Russia gave them real cause to be afraid. These included:
- defeat in war
- shortages of food and supplies
- a disorganised demobilisation
- the overthrow of the monarch
- the setting up of a provisional government
- the establishment of workers' soviets
- preparations for a left-wing coup by extremists, the Spartacists

How close was Germany to revolution?

Despite Ebert's fears, there were a number of differences between the situation in Germany in 1918 and that in Russia in 1917:
- The German working class was much better off than the Russians had been.
- The German middle class was strong and powerful.
- The German army retained much of its morale.
- Conservatism was strong in the civil service and professions.
- The political left was divided.
- The majority of leaders and SDP supporters were not revolutionary.

In view of these differences, you need to ask yourself whether Ebert over-reacted or not, and what the consequences of his actions were.

How did Ebert's response create problems for the future?

The Ebert–Groener Pact with the army provided the support needed to crush the revolutionary soviets, but by using the army and *Freikorps* to defend the republic against threats from groups like the Spartacists, the government increased the power of the military forces. This was to be felt at its most extreme in the right-wing Kapp Putsch in Berlin in March 1920, but the ambitions of the *Freikorps* and innumerable private military groups were to trouble the republic at least until 1923. Some historians have therefore argued that Ebert's exaggeration of the 'revolution', his reliance on the army and right-wing élites, and his suppression of the communists, unwittingly contributed to the eventual failure of the Weimar Republic.

The constitution of the Weimar Republic

The constitution of the new Weimar Republic provides interesting parallels with that of the Second Reich. By preparing a diagram, such as that given opposite, you will see more clearly how the constitution functioned.

PRESIDENT — Head of State
Non-political figure elected every 7 years. Supreme Commander of armed forces. Could summon/dissolve Reichstag. By Article 48, could rule by decree in emergency.

appointed

CHANCELLOR and Cabinet
Chancellor had to have the confidence of the Reichstag and either lead the majority party or be able to negotiate with other leaders to form a workable coalition.

worked with

elected in 'rounds'

REICHSRAT
Nominated by state governments. An advisory body. Could delay, but not veto, legislation.

worked with

REICHSTAG — the sovereign body
Initiated and approved legislation. Elected every 4 years by men and women over 20 years. Chosen from party lists drawn up for whole country. Proportional representation.

elected

LÄNDLER AND STATE GOVERNMENTS
Controlled local state affairs.

elected

elected

GERMAN PEOPLE
Voted for President and elected deputies to Reichstag and state governments.

Compare this diagram with that of the Imperial Constitution of 1871 (p. 14). Make a table to show the similarities and differences.

	Similarities	Differences
Head of government		
Chancellor		
Bundesrat or Reichsrat		
Reichstag		
People		

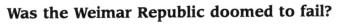

Was the Weimar Republic doomed to fail?

Another theme to consider is whether the Weimar Republic was doomed to fail, or whether it was well established by 1925 and would have been quite capable of surviving but for the repercussions of the Wall Street Crash in 1929. Again, a table will enable you to set out the material for and against the suggestion that it was 'doomed'. A table such as this can make an excellent essay plan.

Years	Doomed to fail?	Well established and likely to survive?
1918–20	Legacy of war — economic problems — shortages and unrest.	War brought to an end and worst problems addressed.
	Versailles Treaty — a damaging blow from the 'November criminals'. Reparations perpetuated economic troubles.	The Versailles treaty was necessary for peace — it was comparatively moderate and the loss of colonial commitments allowed concentration on domestic affairs.
	Left-wing (Spartacists) and right-wing (Kapp Putsch) disturbances.	Disturbances put down and no revolution took place.
	Private military groups created tension.	Ebert–Groener Pact strengthened government and reliance on army necessary.
	Anti-Semitism — murder of Erzberger and Rathenau.	Anti-Semitism was prevalent throughout Europe and did not weaken the Republic.
	Constitutional problems — proportional representation led to weak coalitions.	The constitution vested power in the people of Germany.
	Elites feared workers' legislation while hopes of working class raised unrealistically.	Welfare legislation extended workers' rights and provided a better way of life for the majority.
1923	Economic problems worsened by occupation of the Ruhr. Inflation.	Problems solved by new Rentenmark and inflation cured. The limited unrest showed the stability of the Republic.
	Hitler's Beer Hall Putsch showed how easily circumstances could be exploited.	Nazis failed to gain mass support and were easily crushed.
1924–25	Ruhr occupation left a legacy of bitterness — reparations continued and caused nationalist resentment.	Dawes Plan provided for reorganisation of reparations. Inflation cured.
	Allied troops remained on west bank of Rhine — Germany had not regained any lost land.	French troops withdrew from Ruhr.
	The secret breaking of demilitarisation demands and Stresemann's stance in Europe stored up trouble for future.	Germany became respected abroad.
	Locarno fatefully allowed for revision of eastern borders.	Participated in Locarno Pact (and by 1926 in League of Nations). Stresemann internationally respected.
	Governments were weak, short-lived coalitions in which no party was able to achieve a majority. Government remained unstable.	There were no further coups and democratic parliamentary government seemed well established.
	Hindenburg was elected President and was not committed to parliamentary government.	Hindenburg's election as President reassured conservatives that the Republic would protect their interests.

Review of the content areas

Although it is important to make detailed notes on the content areas specified, do not get so bogged down in detail that you cannot see the wood for the trees. You need to have a clear idea of the basic themes running throughout these three periods of German history. Once you have studied the content areas in some detail, review your material under the following headings, looking at the whole period.

Themes

The economic development of Germany

This was obviously fairly constant despite the political changes, although the policies of individuals (e.g. the introduction of tariffs), factors such as war and reparations, and the changing political condition of Germany are relevant here. You will need to examine the ways in which economic growth conferred power and influence on certain social groups, and what this meant for society and for Germany as a whole.

The development of socialism

The development of socialism as a political force from the time of Bismarck, and its achievements and failures, provides a useful theme. You might also consider whether the establishment of socialist government after the First World War fulfilled the aims of the early socialists.

The political development of Germany

The political development of Germany and the theme of democracy versus authoritarianism are worthy of study. The weaknesses of the constitution of 1871 and the way it developed in the hands of Bismarck and Wilhelm II, when attempts at democracy were combined with authoritarian rule, caused continuing clashes and unease. This remained a problem throughout the war years and although the constitution changed, issues of political power were not entirely resolved by the Weimar Republic. You need to consider the extent to which Germany was a democratic/authoritarian state at the various stages of its development and why its rulers were so frightened by democracy. It would be useful to develop this and look at Germany's political position in comparison with the rest of Europe. Was Germany advanced or backward?

The influence of the military and élites

The influence of the military and of the élites is another recurring theme. Clearly, this was at its greatest in the time of Wilhelm II, but it was already foreshadowed in the days of Bismarck. The Ebert–Groener Pact perpetuated military influence in the years of the Weimar Republic and may be held partly responsible for its difficulties.

Underlying patterns — topic links to the wider specification

This is a self-contained unit, which provides a rewarding period of study in itself. However, the material also provides the basis for the AS Unit 3 of Alternative G, which offers you the opportunity to write one or two course essays on the following topics:

- The Weimar Republic, 1925–33.
- The Nazi consolidation of power, 1930–38.

The issues, areas and themes studied for Unit 1, and in particular political weakness and the interplay of economic and political problems, provide the basis for Unit 3. If you choose to continue with Alternative G in the second year of your course (so moving on to A2), you will find that Unit 1 also provides a foundation for Unit 4. This gives you the opportunity to study:

- The economic modernisation of Germany, 1880–1980.
- The Third Reich and its legacy, 1933–65.

It is not essential to have studied Unit 1 of Alternative G in order to proceed to Unit 4, but it is clearly advantageous to have done so. Even if you choose to move on to a different alternative in the second year of your course, you will still find that the skills developed in AS, particularly the ability to make reasoned and balanced judgements, are relevant. You can complete your study of German history and bring it almost to the present day in Unit 6, when you have the choice of:

- A personal study (which may be set in the context of Alternative G).
- A written paper on the reunification of Germany, 1969-90.

Questions
&
Answers

In Unit 1 you will have to answer two 45-minute questions. The first is compulsory and based on three short source extracts of approximately 200 words. For your second answer you choose between questions 2 or 3. Both of these questions are based on a brief introductory stimulus. All the questions are structured in three parts, as explained in the introduction to this guide, and cover the areas outlined in the Content Guidance section. As there are three main content areas, you can usually expect one question on each area. However, since you do not know which topic will appear in the compulsory question, you cannot afford to leave anything out in your revision.

How to use this section

Two sample papers are given here for you to test your examination skills. You can treat them as individual 'timed' papers, giving you the opportunity for a complete mock examination, or you may like to dip into individual questions as you revise each topic. If you approach the questions in this way, they are divided as follows:

- Germany 1871–90   Paper 1 Question 1 (source question)
                        Paper 2 Question 2

- Germany 1890–1914   Paper 1 Question 2
                        Paper 2 Question 3

- Germany 1914–25   Paper 1 Question 3
                        Paper 2 Question 1 (source question)

When you have attempted each question or paper, you should compare your answers with the candidate response or plan given here. For paper 1, grade A and grade C answers have been provided for every question. Grade A answers should provide a benchmark against which you can compare your work and discover ways of improving on it. The grade C answers will also help you to see some of the potential mistakes that can be made by the average student.

All candidate responses are followed by examiner's comments preceded by the icon *e*. Read these comments carefully and try to get a feel for what is expected. This will help you to improve your performance when you tackle the next question or paper.

For paper 2, a guide as to what might be expected and some comments on possible pitfalls have been provided. Good luck!

Time allowed: 1 hour 30 minutes.

You are advised to spend about 45 minutes on each question.

Answer Question 1 and **either** Question 2 **or** Question 3.

Question 1 Germany, 1871–90

Source A: *Adapted from a speech to the first session of the Imperial Reichstag, 21 March 1871 by Kaiser Wilhelm I*

The honourable calling of the first German Reichstag is to heal the wounds caused by the war and to bestow the gratitude of the Fatherland on those who paid for the victory with their blood or with their lives. At the same time, gentlemen, you will begin the work given to you by the constitution. This means the protection of Germany's existing law and the cultivation of the wellbeing of the German people.

Source B: *From* The Long Nineteenth Century *by David Blackbourn, 1997*

Unification created a sovereign, a nation state with a constitution, a parliament and a German Chancellor. The new Germany included much that was central to liberal programmes such as the rule of law. The National Liberals were the most powerful political party in Germany by the end of the unification process. The 1870s represented, in many ways, a liberal high point in nineteenth-century Germany. The Reichstag was elected by a franchise that was universal, direct and equal for males over the age of 25. The elections were almost entirely free of interference. A party system emerged. The 1870s was a crucial decade of consolidation.

Source C: *From* Bismarck *by B. Waller, 1985*

What Imperial Germany did not have was parliamentary government. The parliament had very extensive powers, but it lacked one which was crucial. The Chancellor was not responsible to parliament, but rather to the upper chamber and the Emperor. To be enacted, laws had to receive his approval, and that of both houses of parliament as well. Of course Bismarck had the upper hand and used it occasionally.

(a) Study Source A. Using your own knowledge, explain briefly the importance of 'the war' in the context of the summoning of the first Imperial Reichstag.   (3 marks)

(b) Study Sources B and C. With reference to your own knowledge, explain how the view of parliamentary government put forward in Source C challenges that put forward in Source B.   (7 marks)

(c) Study Sources A, B, and C and use your own knowledge. In what ways did the Imperial Constitution of 1871, and Bismarck's attitude as Chancellor, prevent the development of effective parliamentary government in Germany to 1890?   (15 marks)

Total: 25 marks

■ ■ ■

Answer to paper 1, question 1: grade C candidate

(a) Bismarck fought three wars to unify Germany: a war with Denmark over Schleswig-Holstein, a war with Austria and a war with France. Many were killed in these wars and 'paid for the victory with their blood or with their lives'. The French army was trapped at Metz and Napoleon III was forced to surrender at Sedan. The wars ended when Paris was forced to surrender. After the wars Germany was unified with a Reichstag to govern it.

> *e* This answer has failed to keep to the point of the question — a common error. It shows an understanding of how Bismarck united Germany by war (the importance of war), but gives too much detail. Only the war with France is relevant here, and it would have been better if the candidate could have supplied some dates (there is even a clue in the dating of the source). Details of the French war are also unnecessary and the quotation from the source adds nothing since the question says 'using your own knowledge...'. The candidate would receive credit for pointing out that the war led to unification (the context) and showing some (even rudimentary) awareness of what the Reichstag was. This answer would gain 2 out of 3 marks, but the same mark could have been obtained by supplying the first and last sentences only.

(b) Source C says what Imperial Germany did not have was parliamentary government. It says the parliament had very extensive powers but it lacked a crucial one. The Chancellor was not responsible to Parliament. He was chosen by the upper chamber and the Emperor. He had to approve laws and that meant he was very powerful and Bismarck always got his own way.

Source B says that Germany did have a parliament after unification and that the National Liberals were the most important political party. The Reichstag was elected by male franchise over 25 and the elections were free.

The author of Source C doesn't think that the German Parliament was very effective. He is right because although there were elections and parties in the Reichstag, it could not make laws on its own. The Bundesrat could refuse to pass laws, and Prussia controlled it anyway. The Reichstag could do nothing that Prussia, which included the Emperor and the Chancellor, disapproved of. The Emperor also had great powers of his own. He appointed the Chancellor and controlled the army.

e This candidate has adopted a very poor, but unfortunately all too common, approach. He has summarised what each source says, almost word for word, without comparing. He would gain some credit for extracting the relevant information, but otherwise this is worth very little. Only in the final section does he begin to answer the question, showing some 'own knowledge'. However, the knowledge is accurate and appropriate, although the conclusion is not fully developed. This answer would gain 4/7 marks.

(c) Germany had a parliament called the Bundesrat and the Reichstag. Source A tells us that the duty of the Reichstag was the protection of law and the wellbeing of the German people. Source B talks about the rule of law. Source B also tells us that the Reichstag was elected by a franchise that was universal, direct and equal for males over 25. The elections were free from interference. There was also a party system. Source C says that although parliament had very extensive powers, the Chancellor was not responsible to parliament. Laws had to receive the approval of both houses of parliament and the Chancellor, Bismarck, had a lot of influence.

At first Bismark allied with the National Liberals in the Reichstag in a fight against the Catholics called the Kulturkampf. Bismarck was frightened that the Catholics were more loyal to Pope Pius IX, who had said that he was infallible, than to the new state of Germany. He passed the May Laws against the Catholics. In 1872 he banned the Jesuits from Germany and in 1873 he passed laws to give the government control over the appointment of priests. The National Liberals supported him and the constitution was quite effective.

The Kulturkampf was not a success and the Centre Party grew stronger instead of weaker. This alarmed Bismarck. At the same time there was an economic depression and the Conservatives wanted an end to free trade to protect the Junkers. Bismarck wanted a law against the growing Socialist Party and so in 1878 he abandoned his alliance with the Liberals and allied instead with the Conservatives. He introduced tariffs which pleased the Conservatives and he was reasonably successful.

As well as passing laws against the Socialists, Bismarck introduced his own 'state socialism' in the 1880s, with sickness and accident insurance and old age pensions. He thought the workers would be grateful and stop supporting the Socialist Party, but this didn't work any better than his campaign against the Catholics. The party continued to grow.

Bismarck did not like parliamentary government and he kept a firm control over parliament until he was dismissed in 1890 because of disagreements with the new Kaiser, Wilhelm II. The new Emperor was young and thought he knew how to run Germany better than Bismarck who was by then an old man. He was wrong and things in Germany got more out of control until Germany found itself at war in 1914.

 This answer refers both to the sources and to 'own knowledge' and it contains a good deal of accurate and relevant information. It shows some understanding, covers the whole period, and shows how Bismarck ruled in the years 1871–90.

On the other hand, there is a limited amount of explicit reference to the question. Although the candidate has selected relevant information, there is a good deal of narrative and the crucial issue of how Bismarck retained control through a series of political manoeuvres is lost in the detail. The obvious conclusion, that the Reichstag must have had considerable power if Bismarck felt it necessary to ensure he had allies there, is never made. The candidate also gives unnecessary details of the Kulturkampf and Bismarck's 'state socialism', although this has some relevance to 'Bismarck's attitude'.

The ending, typical of a candidate who has not focused well on the question, is also poor. The final sentence should be a direct statement in response to the question — not a vague speculation about what was to come.

This answer would receive 8/15 marks because it lacks weight and balance, and despite implicit understanding it is mainly dependent on description. It has some valid links to the question and is coherent in structure, but it has not really addressed all the issues raised by the question.

■ ■ ■

Answer to paper 1, question 1: grade A candidate

(a) The war refers to the Franco–Prussian War of 1870–71, in which Prussia forced the southern German States to join forces with the Prussian-dominated North German Confederation to defeat their common enemy, France. This brought about the final unification of Germany. Wilhelm I was proclaimed Emperor of the united Germany at Versailles on 18 January 1871, and a constitution was drawn up giving Germany two assemblies, a Bundesrat and a Reichstag, elected by all males over the age of 25.

This is an impressive answer, well worth 3/3 marks. It would not be necessary to include all this information in a 3-mark answer, but a candidate who can produce a direct and detailed response such as this, in three sentences, is assured of full marks. Its merits are that 'the war' is precisely identified; the 'importance' of the war is clearly shown in the reference to the southern states and unification; and there is an excellent understanding of 'context' with both the constitution and the Reichstag briefly explained. (Note that the candidate has made use of some relevant information in Source B about the franchise. He may have known this anyway, but by reading all the sources it is sometimes possible to pick up useful information.)

(b) While the view of Source B is that the growth of parliamentary government, which established the 'rule of law', was an important step forward in Germany and led to a 'liberal high point', the view of Source C is that there were several things wrong with the new constitution. Firstly, the Chancellor and both houses of parliament had to give their assent before a law could be made, and secondly, the Reichstag could not get rid of the Chancellor who was only responsible to the Emperor and the Bundesrat.

There is some truth in both viewpoints. There were a number of limitations to the German Constitution, and the elected Reichstag could be over-ruled by the Prussian-dominated Bundesrat. However, there was a wide franchise, a reasonably fair 'rule of law', and the parties in the Reichstag could debate major issues. As Chancellor, Bismarck 'had the upper hand', as Source C points out, but he still had to put a lot of effort into controlling and winning support in the Reichstag.

Source C takes quite a narrow view of the working of the constitution, looking primarily at the power of the Chancellor. Source B, on the other hand, ignores the limitations and looks at the wider implications of the development of parliamentary government and liberal ideas. Both sources are rather one-sided, but much evidence, for example of the debates in the Reichstag over free trade or socialism, supports the view of Source B, that the new constitution did help create parliamentary government in Germany.

> ✏ This answer is very well structured and includes some comment, which is vital for the highest marks. Remember that it does not matter which viewpoint is taken, as long as there is some attempt at supported evaluation. This candidate has identified how the sources differ and has shown why he finds one more convincing than the other. This answer would receive 7/7 marks.

(c) The Imperial Constitution of 1871 and Bismarck's attitude as Chancellor from 1871–90 placed severe limits on the development of effective parliamentary government. Not only did the constitution ensure the dominance of Prussia and in particular of its chief minister, Bismarck, who became Chancellor of the new Empire, it also placed clear restraints on the position of the Reichstag, the lower, elected house. Although Kaiser Wilhelm I's speech to the first Reichstag, given in Source A, hints that the Reichstag had much power and an important future, 'you will begin the work given to you...the protection of law...the cultivation of the wellbeing of the...people', in practice its position was limited and its dealings deliberately restricted by Bismarck.

The provisions of the constitution provided a parliamentary structure with two Houses but it placed limits on their power. The Upper House, or Bundesrat, was made up of men appointed by the 25 states of the Empire, in proportion to their size and population. Prussia, as the largest state, had 17 representatives. Bavaria, the next largest, had 6. The Bundesrat could initiate legislation, and with the permission of the Emperor could declare war and settle disputes between states.

It met in private and was chaired by Bismarck, the Chancellor, or the Kaiser. These facts say a good deal about the limitations of the constitution. Both the Kaiser and Chancellor were Prussian, and since 14 votes were needed to veto legislation, Prussia had effective control. The Kaiser chose his own ministers and these usually came from the Bundesrat, which in effect was the real centre of government.

However, the constitution had some democratic features and it might have been expected to produce effective parliamentary government. Although legislation began in the Bundesrat, it also needed the consent of the Reichstag. As described in Source B, this was freely elected by universal manhood suffrage for the over 25s and so, in theory, represented the wishes of the people. Indeed, it contained a wide variety of political parties, as also noted in Source B, and represented a range of German political interests. Most important of all, it had to approve the budget, which laid down what the government would raise in taxes and how it would spend them every year. This was a very significant power.

Yet it would be wrong to describe the workings of the Imperial Constitution of 1871 as a full parliamentary democracy. The Reichstag was subject to the whims of the Bundesrat, the government ministers and the Chancellor, over whom, as Source C points out, it had no direct control. Although the Reichstag might question the Chancellor and debate points of his policy, there was no need for the ministers to pay any attention to its suggestions. The Chancellor and ministers remained aloof from the party system, so although 'a party system emerged' as noted in Source B, the party that had attracted the most votes in the elections still played no direct role in drawing up government policy. Karl Liebknecht, a left-wing socialist, described the constitution as a sham, 'a fig leaf covering the nakedness of absolutism'.

The attitude of Bismarck, as Chancellor, also helped prevent the development of effective parliamentary government. He viewed the Reichstag as a body to be manipulated rather than as a house whose views were to be adopted as the will of the German people. Consequently, he never encouraged parliamentary government. On several occasions he even suggested, half seriously, that the powers of the Reichstag should be cut or destroyed, and he once complained to a friend that the Germans were ruining the toy he had given them to play with.

One example of the way Bismarck curbed the growth of parliamentary government can be seen in his fight to retain control of military spending. Although the approval of the budget was an important right of the Reichstag, in 1874 he persuaded the house to vote away part of this right by agreeing to debate the military budget only every 7 years. This was repeated in 1881 and 1887, and according to Hajo Holborn the 'loss of the full right of budget approval blocked the growth of a parliamentary system in Germany'. Since much of the Reich's income came, in any case, from indirect taxation and the contributions of the various member states, the Reichstag's financial control was therefore as limited as Bismarck dared to make it.

Bismarck's attitude as Chancellor prevented the development of effective parliamentary government in other ways too. Although he knew that he could not ignore the Reichstag since he needed it to pass legislation, he looked for ways to win support for his own views, by balancing groups one against another rather than going along with the policies of the majority of the deputies. He worked with alliances, such as that with the National Liberals to 1878, and the Conservative alliance from 1879–90. He altered his support for parties as it suited him, and those who dared speak against him in the Reichstag were deemed 'Reichsfeinde', or enemies of the state.

When the composition of the Reichstag was not to Bismarck's liking, he used elections to get a more amenable one. So, for example, when he wanted to end the Liberal alliance in 1878, he used the excuse of two assassination attempts on the Kaiser to launch an attack on the 'unpatriotic Liberals', who had refused to pass an anti-Socialist law. Similarly, in 1887, following a row over the army estimates, Bismarck called an election and played on fears of war with France to ensure the return of a loyal 'Kartell' of Conservatives and National Liberals to support him. By measures such as these, Bismarck carried through the legislation he wanted and Reichstag members accepted, for the most part, that their role was confined to criticism, not any serious attempt to increase power. This is far from 'effective parliamentary government'. Some historians even speak of Bismarck exerting a 'personal dictatorship' by the 1880s, although this seems an exaggeration since his opponents, the Centre Party and SPD, were still powerful and able to criticise.

Effective parliamentary government was therefore stifled, partly by the Imperial Constitution with its many restrictions, partly by Bismarck's attitude as Chancellor, and partly by the Reichstag's own willingness to submit. This is perhaps unsurprising given Prussian tradition and the divisions within the Reichstag which made effective coalitions in opposition to government policy difficult. The Centre Party formed in 1871 split the natural middle-class vote, while the National Liberals were destroyed as a united force after 1878. So, although there were many signs in Bismarck's Germany of a modern state which allowed people to express their views, and there would not have been so much interest in the elections had the Reichstag counted for nothing at all, nevertheless, in the face of Bismarck's determination and political skill, there was little chance of 'effective parliamentary government' developing. Bismarck was largely to blame for the direction in which parliamentary politics went in the years 1871–90.

🖉 Although rather lengthy, this is a stylish and convincing answer. The examiner is immediately impressed by the direct introduction, which clearly focuses on the question. This is followed by a knowledgeable analysis of the Imperial Constitution which refers to both sources and 'own knowledge'. Notice how effectively the sources are used. Their points are not simply listed but carefully woven into the fabric of the answer. The essay follows a clear structure. Each paragraph begins with a reference to the question and all the material is carefully chosen to relate to the question. The democratic features of the constitution are balanced against the undemocratic, and a survey of Bismarck's attitude to the Reichstag is followed by examples of the way he curbed its power. Details of his policies are only given where relevant to support the argument. Appropriate quotations are skilfully used to add weight to some of the points made. The answer ends with a focused conclusion, which picks up the points made in the answer, tries to balance factors and offers some judgement. The whole answer is written in an accurate, fluent style and would be well worth 15/15 marks.

Question 2 Germany, 1890–1914

Read the following source and then answer the questions which follow:

In the Germany of Wilhelm II, power was concentrated in the hands of the élites. They did not necessarily hold office but they had sufficient money and influence to ensure that their views were not only heard, but acted upon.

(a) **What is meant by the élites in Wilhelm II's Germany?** (3 marks)

(b) **Explain the ways in which the élites influenced policy in this period.** (7 marks)

(c) **'Germany after 1890 became an increasingly autocratic state in which the personal influence of Kaiser Wilhelm II was decisive.' Explain why you agree or disagree with this statement.** (15 marks)

Total: 25 marks

Answer to paper 1, question 2: grade C candidate

(a) The élites were the Junker landowners. They came from Prussia and had huge estates. Men with money and influence, like the Junkers, forced their views on the government of Wilhelm II.

> This answer partly repeats what the extract says and only identifies the élites with Junker landowners, although in the third sentence it hints that they were just one of the élite groups influencing government. This is barely a grade C answer and would gain only 1/3 marks.

(b) The élites were the friends of Kaiser Wilhelm II and they supported the sort of military policies he favoured. One of these was Weltpolitik which was the search for world power. Through the Agrarian and Colonial Leagues they campaigned for more colonies as German businessmen wanted more colonies as markets for their goods and to supply them with raw materials. Their ideas were supported by Wilhelm II and the army. This policy is called the search for a place in the sun because Germany expanded into Africa and took parts of the coast of China and this meant that Germany needed a bigger navy which the business men wanted too because they needed ships to protect their trading fleets and the military men wanted to show Germany's power so Weltpolitik also led to the Naval Laws of 1898 and 1900 which shows the influence of the élites.

The army was another élite group in Germany and soldiers seemed to be able to do as they liked. Trouble broke out in Zabern in 1913 because Alsace had been annexed in 1871 and the army was on bad terms with the inhabitants. The soldiers stationed there behaved badly and there was a demonstration against them. The soldiers acted brutally when they tried to disperse the crowds and arrested 28 citizens, including a judge and a lawyer and imprisoned them overnight in the barracks. This was illegal and there were civil rights protests against the soldiers' actions throughout Germany. However, when the Kaiser was asked to deal with the complaints, he refused and supported the soldiers and gave the impression that they could do anything. This shows how influential the army élite had become.

> *e* This answer is not very well written. The sentence structure is poor and in places this almost obscures the meaning; in the first paragraph the candidate has also made the mistake of writing Agrarian League instead of Pan-German League. Nevertheless, it does introduce two relevant ideas about the ways in which the élites influenced policy in Germany, and it makes the point that the élites' influence came about through the coincidence of their views with those of the Kaiser. The two areas mentioned are reasonably full, although some of the details of *Weltpolitik* are not well related to the question and the account of the Zabern incident is largely narrative. Unfortunately, the candidate has not gone on to develop other examples of élite influence, or to link the points made, and the answer is rather narrow in both range and comment. It would receive 4/7 marks.

(c) I agree, Germany did become an increasingly autocratic state after 1890 and the personal influence of Kaiser Wilhelm II was decisive. Wilhelm was arrogant and self-opinionated. He often said things without thinking of the consequences, as in the 'Daily Telegraph' interview of 1908, or the Zabern Affair of 1913. He liked constant praise and flattery and attracted a strange mixture of 'friends'.

Germany was dominated by two important groups — the nobility and the army. The soldiers took an oath of loyalty directly to the Kaiser and army officers became very influential at the Kaiser's court. He even told the army, 'we belong to each other'. The army and nobility were linked by family ties and through their contact with the Kaiser.

Although Germany was meant to be a democracy and the people elected deputies for the Reichstag, it did not have much effect on the Kaiser. Even after 1912, when the socialists became the largest party in the Reichstag, they couldn't influence policies. They opposed many of the taxes which the Kaiser asked for, but despite the arguments he got his own way.

The Kaiser played a huge part in the way Germany developed after 1890. He was really only interested in military matters, Weltpolitik and making Germany strong and respected abroad. It has been said that his concern for foreign policy and German national greatness was his way of distracting the people from their internal problems. If this is true the First World War was the result of Wilhelm's failure to understand the real needs of Germany.

> *e* This answer shows an understanding of the personal influence of the Kaiser, and even includes the influence of the élites. However, it is underdeveloped and fails to consider the first part of the quotation on how government and the state were becoming increasingly autocratic. It makes no attempt to show how the statement could be disputed. This is an easy mistake to make if the question is not read carefully and a short plan prepared before beginning the answer. While there is therefore some understanding of one aspect of the question shown, the answer is incomplete, limited in argument and lacking in weight and balance. It therefore only just merits a borderline C grade, 8/15 marks.

■ ■ ■

Answer to paper 1, question 2: grade A candidate

(a) The élite groups were the landowning Prussian Junkers and large industrialists whose wealth and status gave them a forceful influence over policy making. They dominated the army and administration and helped shape conservative policies. They were strengthened by pressure groups such as the Pan-German League, the Agrarian League and the Colonial League.

> *e* In three sentences the élites are defined, their importance explained in the context of Kaiser Wilhelm II's reign, and the pressure groups mentioned. This would ensure a mark of 3/3.

(b) The élites influenced policy by placing pressure on the Kaiser to protect their interests and they were generally successful in dominating government. For example, because the landowning Junkers feared Chancellor Caprivi's interest in social problems, they encouraged the Kaiser to dismiss him. After this they combined with the industrialist élites in 'Sammlungspolitik' and, with the help of the Agrarian League, forced the reintroduction of tariffs. The combined élite groups, with the support of the Pan-German and Colonial leagues, favoured Weltpolitik. This appealed to the nationalist Junkers who gloried in 'world power', and also met the demand of German industry for new resources and markets. The industrial interests similarly welcomed Germany's naval building programme, which provided them with orders. Some historians believe that the élites favoured Weltpolitik as a way of distracting the middle and working classes from social and political problems at home.

The army was a particularly powerful élite group. When they behaved in an irresponsible way against the citizens of Zabern in 1913, the pro-military Kaiser ignored the outcry in the Reichstag and took no disciplinary action against them. The military élites also drew up the irresponsible Schlieffen Plan as a strategy to avoid a war on two fronts. Since this involved a sweep through Belgium, and Germany had been one of the guarantors of Belgian neutrality, the plan was morally wrong, but no one in Germany dared criticise it. Both these examples suggest that the army élite could do as it pleased.

There were, of course, other influences on policy in these years — particularly the growing SPD, which did its best to counter the influence of the élites. However, it is fair to conclude that German policy was very much influenced by the power of the various élite groups and above all the army. This was undoubtedly because of the attitude of the Kaiser. Since his interests and ambitions, at least from 1894, coincided with those of the élites, and in particular the army, it is not surprising that they had so much influence.

This is a very full answer and longer than might be expected for a 7-mark question. However, it keeps to the point and there are many appropriate comments on the information provided. The answer gives a range of ways in which the élites influenced policy and it provides a neat, well-balanced ending. It links the various points together, showing awareness of other factors that influenced policy and concluding that in this case Wilhelm II's personal interest was important in furthering the power of the élites. It would obtain a top mark of 7/7.

(c) There is plenty of evidence to support the view that Kaiser Wilhelm II exerted a major influence over the development of German policy after 1890, and that his personal interventions led German government along an increasingly autocratic path. Not all historians agree with this view. The German historian Wehler, for example, described Wilhelm II as only a 'shadow Emperor' and said that he merely made speeches while real power was in the hands of the élites. However, it is hard to dismiss the role of the Kaiser, and other historians, such as Röhl, have convincingly argued that he was decisive in shaping German policy and the autocratic nature of the state.

Kaiser Wilhelm II had a very firm belief in his right to rule and his decision-making ability. He once wrote in a letter, 'I am guided only by my duty and the responsibility of my clear conscience towards God.' However, despite his arrogance, he never fully understood the demands of policy making, nor was he prepared to listen to others. He liked obedience and did not take kindly to criticism. He disliked working with civilians, and regarded himself as a soldier, spending much of his time with military friends. He normally only met his Chancellor once a week but he saw the Chief of the Military Cabinet three times weekly! His personality and interests therefore go some way towards explaining the increasingly autocratic tendencies in German government after 1890.

Bismarck's constitution of 1871 had left the Emperor with considerable powers.

He had absolute control over the government, the armed forces, the diplomatic corps and the civil service. Wilhelm II used these powers to appoint those he favoured to high office. These were men who were prepared to support and flatter him, rather than those with ability. He chose Chancellors he believed he could influence — first Caprivi, an army general who was soon dismissed when he showed a will of his own, then Hohenlohe who was elderly and only a figure head. Chancellor Bülow was nicknamed 'the eel' because of the way he ingratiated himself with the Emperor, while Bethmann-Hollweg was chosen because he would not interfere with Wilhelm II's foreign ambitions. It was, of course, disastrous to have Chancellors who could not control the Reichstag, and thanks to Wilhelm II's influence, controversial domestic policies, such as social reform, were largely ignored, and government concentrated on foreign affairs. This was the sign of an increasingly autocratic state.

Kaiser Wilhelm certainly had an autocratic outlook and even those chosen by him, like Caprivi, could not rely on his support. He liked to decide things himself and could fly into fits of rage if he did not get his own way. He became very determined when he wanted a particular policy, for example, in the fight for the Army Bill of 1891–93. He also led the crusade against the socialists in 1894–95 and made hysterical speeches demanding a battle against the 'parties of revolution'. His obsession with naval expansion from 1895 onwards was another indication of his determination to have his own way, and his commitment also contributed towards the decision to go to war in 1914.

The autocratic tendencies of Wilhelm II led to some disastrous interference. He was responsible for ruining Germany's relations with Great Britain by his ill-considered actions and statements. The Krüger telegram (1895) directed against the British, and the 'Daily Telegraph' interview of 1908 when he aired views about German attitudes and intentions towards Britain without reference to the Reichstag, gave the impression of an autocratic ruler behaving as he wished and ignoring the voice of the people's elected representatives. Similarly, the Zabern incident of 1913 showed that Wilhelm II believed that he could rule in an authoritarian way, refusing to discipline the military who had abused their authority over the local townsfolk, despite the outcry in Germany. His actions amounted to an assertion that the army was above the law — and that any group that had the Emperor's support could do as it liked.

There is plenty of evidence, therefore, to support the view that Kaiser Wilhelm II's personal influence did help make Germany an increasingly autocratic state. However, that is not quite the whole picture. It must not be forgotten that Germany did have a Parliament — a Reichstag and a Bundesrat, and that the elected Reichstag did show some power. They forced the rejection of bills, for example Hohenlöhe's anti-socialist legislation, so the Kaiser could not always get what he wanted. From 1907–09 Bülow became the first Chancellor to rule with the backing of a fixed group of parties, a fact which shows the government needed to have Reichstag support. The Socialists continued to increase their influence, despite the Kaiser's views, and they became the largest party in the Reichstag by 1912. So, despite the absolutist tendencies, Germany was still a parliamentary government, although the influence of Wilhelm II had done nothing to promote this, and in many respects, the autocratic tendencies were far more in evidence.

e This answer shows a good understanding of the question. It is particularly impressive that some historiography has been introduced to support the differing opinions of Wilhelm II's influence (although Wehler's views are simply dismissed). From the outset, the candidate makes it clear that there are two sides to this question. There is a good analysis of Wilhelm II's influence in government, with plenty of relevant examples. The answer looks at his personality, his powers and the uses to which he put these, before concluding that he did increase the autocratic tendencies of government but that the basic parliamentary structure remained intact. This is a thoughtful answer which would deserve full marks (15/15).

Question 3 Germany, 1914–25

Read the following source and then answer the questions which follow:

> Munich was the centre of violent political upheaval in postwar Germany. First came Kurt Eisner's socialist republic, Bavaria's contribution to the 'German revolution' of 1918–19. There followed an ultra-right-wing political regime, and in November 1923, Hitler's bid for power in the 'Beer Hall Putsch'.

(a) **What is meant by 'Kurt Eisner's socialist republic' in the context of the 'German revolution' of 1918–19?** (3 marks)

(b) **Explain how the Weimar Republic survived the threat of left- and right-wing revolts in 1918–23.** (7 marks)

(c) **Do you agree that economic problems were the prime cause of instability in the Weimar Republic to 1925? Explain your answer.** (15 marks)

Total: 25 marks

■ ■ ■

Answer to paper 1, question 3: grade C candidate

(a) Kurt Eisner set up a socialist republic in Munich, in the north of Germany, at the time of the German Revolution of 1918–19. This was yet another challenge to the government, which faced left- and right-wing revolts at the end of the war.

📝 This answer merely repeats information that is given in the source, pointing out that 'this was yet another challenge to the government' and showing a minimal awareness of the political troubles in Germany at this time. The candidate also adds inaccurate information on the location of Munich (which is actually in the south of Germany) — a silly mistake. The candidate would gain 1/3 marks for basic understanding of 1918–19, but nothing more.

(b) In 1918, the army promised to support the Republic and crush revolutionaries. It dealt firmly with the Spartacists who attempted a rising in Berlin in 1919. After 3 days of street fighting the Spartacists were crushed and their leaders, Karl Liebknecht and Rosa Luxemburg, were killed. The Republic had survived the threat from the left.

In 1920, some of the army called the Freikorps began a revolt under their leader, Kapp. This time the Weimar government was forced to leave Berlin, because it had no army to protect it. It appealed to the workers to come out on strike. The general strike defeated the Kapp Putsch and that threat from the right was destroyed.

In 1923 Hitler led the Beer Hall Putsch. This was another right-wing attempt to seize power. Hitler marched his men through the streets of Munich, shouting abuse at the government, but he did not win a great deal of support, and his rebellion was easily crushed and he was captured. The Weimar Republic never realised what a threat Hitler was and they even treated him quite leniently after he was captured, allowing him to write 'Mein Kampf' while in prison. By 1923 the Weimar Republic had survived the threat of left- and right-wing revolts with the use of the army and the workers and now, under Stresemann, the Republic was able to enjoy its 'golden years' before the Wall Street Crash created further gloom.

📝 This answer shows a reasonable understanding of how the Republic relied on the army to crush left-wing revolts, although it muddles the army (the regular *Reichswehr*) and the *Freikorps*. It also refers to the way the right-wing Kapp Putsch was destroyed, but it does not really explain why Hitler's Beer Hall Putsch failed, although it does mention lack of support. The details of the march, Hitler's lenient punishment and *Mein Kampf* are irrelevant, and the concluding comments could be fuller. Overall, the answer would merit 4/7 marks; it mentions a few ways in which the Weimar Republic was able to survive, but does not make any effective links between these or provide a convincing conclusion.

(c) The Weimar Republic's main economic problems were reparations and hyper-inflation. At the Versailles Peace Conference it was decided that Germany would pay reparations, as a sort of fine, to the Allies for all the damage Germany had done in the war. The Allies were angry with Germany, especially Clemenceau of France who was determined to prevent Germany from becoming a strong power again. He wanted to punish Germany as harshly as possible and Lloyd George, although more moderate, had been elected with slogans like 'make Germany pay'. But were economic problems the prime cause of instability? First we need to examine exactly what those economic problems were. Only by looking at the economic problems in detail can we find out whether they caused instability or not.

A reparations committee was set up that eventually decided on the amount Germany would have to pay — £6,600 million! This led to an appalling economic situation in Germany. The French government soon complained that Germany was behind with payments and in 1923 the French sent troops into the Ruhr to try to force her to pay. The idea was that the troops would occupy this industrial area and take the coal, iron and steel themselves instead of payments. This caused a major economic crisis and the government tried to undermine the French efforts by telling the workers to go on strike. The result was a decline in German industry and a fall in the value of the mark — hyperinflation. Now we must consider how this caused problems in Germany.

Hyperinflation is when prices go up really fast. The government printed masses of paper money to try to cope, but the money became worthless. Children were playing with banknotes, and people needed wheelbarrows full to buy small items like a loaf of bread. This was a very difficult time for the Weimar Republic. The German people blamed the reparations and the Republic. It looked as though Weimar had brought nothing but chaos. In Bavaria Hitler led the Beer Hall Putsch in protest against the 'November criminals' who had signed the Treaty of Versailles. However, things got better after Stresemann took control. He ended the strike in the Ruhr and issued a new currency called the Rentenmark which stopped all the inflation.

We must now return to the question of whether economic troubles were the prime cause of instability for the Weimar Republic. How did they affect the political situation which the government faced? The Republic faced many threats from the left and right wing. The left-wing Spartacists Rising in 1919, the attempt at a communist republic in Bavaria and the right-wing Kapp Putsch in 1920 all took place during the economic troubles immediately after the war when there were food shortages. Hitler's Beer Hall Putsch also took place during the hyperinflation of 1923. It is therefore clear that economic problems were the prime cause of instability in the Weimar Republic.

🖉 This answer is poorly constructed and mainly dependent on description. However, it contains a good deal of relevant information on the economic problems of the Weimar Republic, and highlights the most important of these quite well. There is some implicit reference to economic problems promoting instability, notably in the reference to Hitler's Munich Putsch. Any explicit connection between economic troubles and instability is left until the conclusion, and even here the linking of the troubles of 1919–20 and economic problems (only food shortages are mentioned) is not very convincing. The answer therefore shows limited understanding; the acceptance, without question, that economic problems were the prime cause of instability also means that the answer is not well balanced. In addition, it stops in 1923, not 1925.

The impression given is made worse by the style of writing, which includes much 'scaffolding', particularly in the first and last paragraphs. Sentences which relate what 'we' must do, rather than getting on and doing it, serve no purpose. The phrase 'we must now return to the question' is almost an admission that much of the answer has strayed from the point. Avoid this irritating style of writing. You will not impress any examiner in this way. This answer would gain a C grade, 9/15 marks.

◼ ◼ ◼

Answer to paper 1, question 3: grade A candidate

(a) In November 1918, Kurt Eisner, a former journalist and leading member of the USPD, the left-wing Independent Socialist Party, attempted to set up a council of workers and soldiers in Munich to control Bavarian affairs. This was part of the 'German Revolution' which began in October 1918 with naval mutinies in Wilhelmshaven and Kiel, the establishment of workers' councils throughout Germany and riots in the Ruhr. Eisner's regime soon collapsed (as did the 'revolution') and he was murdered in February 1919.

> This is a full answer. It identifies Eisner and explains what happened to him and his regime. The information is set in the context of the German Revolution, which is itself also clearly explained. It would receive 3/3 marks.

(b) The Weimar government took several crucial steps to survive the threats from left and right. Firstly, in November 1918, Chancellor Ebert made a pact with General Groener. This provided support from the army which then crushed the revolutionary soviets that had been set up across Germany. The 'Freikorps', mainly ex-servicemen under the control of former army officers, helped stamp out left-wing revolts, such as the Spartacists' Rebellion in Berlin in January 1919. The army also helped destroy Eisner's socialist republic in Bavaria and a communist rising in the Ruhr in 1920.

Ebert gained the support of the workers by setting up a 'central working association' to establish trade union negotiating rights and an 8 hour day. This proved another crucial step for the Republic's survival. In March 1920, a group of officers led by Wolfgang Kapp attempted to overthrow the government in Berlin. The Reichswehr refused to act against this right-wing putsch, but the German workers defended the Republic and destroyed the putsch with a general strike.

Throughout the early 1920s the Republic faced both left- and right-wing disturbances. The 'white terror' was organised by the Freikorps and other paramilitary groups such as the Stahelm and Hitler's Sturmabteilung, and there were political assassinations such as that of Erzberger and Rathenau. The government tried to deal with this by setting up special courts to prosecute those involved in violence. However, in 1923, Stresemann was forced to ask President Ebert to use Article 48 of the constitution and declare a state of national emergency. Once again the army saved the Republic. It destroyed the 'Black Reichswehr' and the communist paramilitaries, while in Bavaria the police suppressed Hitler's Beer Hall Putsch.

Between 1918 and 1923 the Weimar government took a number of steps to survive the crises it faced, but of these undoubtedly the most important was the pact with the army. This provided the power and support the Republic needed and although it added to the confidence of the right, without it the Republic might not have survived at all.

> ✏ This answer demonstrates a good understanding of a range of material. It links the revolts to the government's actions and it supplies an appropriate conclusion, stressing the importance of the pact with the army over other factors. It would merit 7/7 marks.

(c) Economic problems were certainly a major cause of instability for the Weimar Republic. The Republic was born in 1918 at the end of a war that had left Germany in a dire economic position. The British blockade of her ports had caused severe disruption to food supplies, and clothing, fuel and other essentials were all in short supply. Strikes in protest against the continuation of the war and an influenza epidemic that year had made matters worse, and the 'German Revolution' of 1918–19, with naval mutinies and left-wing attempts to seize power, was partly a response to these economic troubles.

The economic collapse was made worse by the loss of major economic resources such as those of Alsace-Lorraine and the colonies at Versailles and the Allies' decision to impose economic reparations on Germany. Such humiliation added fuel to the protests of right-wing groups, and in particular the paramilitary groups and Freikorps which were behind much of the instability of the early 20s in their clashes with the left. When the first finance minister, Matthias Erzberger, tried to cope by introducing a system of progressive taxation together with taxes on profits and inherited wealth, there was such an outcry that he was forced into retirement in 1920.

When Germany failed to deliver an interim payment in March 1921, Allied troops crossed the Rhine. In April 1921 the Allies fixed reparations at 132,000 million gold marks over 30 years which was an astronomical amount given Germany's circumstances. Despite the efforts of Wirth, the new finance minister, to win a reduction in the demands or a 2 year postponement, both were refused and in January 1923, when Germany fell behind with payments, the French occupied the Ruhr. This accelerated Germany's economic collapse by triggering a massive rise in inflation, and industry came to a standstill. The inflationary crisis added to the unrest and provided fuel for the extremists. Right-wing rebels, such as Hitler, blamed the crisis at different times on the Jews, the Versailles Treaty, the Weimar politicians and the Socialists.

However, despite the massive economic unrest, the radical right-wing did not win extensive popular support. This is probably because, grave though the problems were, for many working people the monetary crisis was quite short-lived.

Stresemann became Chancellor in August 1923 and stopped the policy of passive resistance in the Ruhr in September. He promised to start paying reparations again to ease the international situation and was therefore able to tackle hyperinflation. He appointed Schacht who issued a new currency, the Rentenmark, in November and so put the mark on a new firm footing. He also negotiated the Dawes Plan of 1924 which reorganised the system of reparations and provided a loan to help stabilise the economy. Such measures restored confidence, and it is significant that as the economic troubles receded, so did the political violence. There were no attempted coups from the right or left from 1924 to 1929.

However, economic problems were not the sole cause of Germany's instability. There were many other factors such as defeat and humiliation in war and the example of the Communist revolution in Russia 1917, which inspired the political left. Separatism was an issue in the troubles in Bavaria and the inexperience of the Weimar politicians, and the multiplicity of political parties permitted by the Weimar constitution in a country used to strong authoritarian government weakened the control from the top. The fact that the new rulers were branded 'traitors' by those angered by the 'capitulation' to the Allies' harsh peace terms (including war guilt and the dismantling of the armed forces) did not help either. Even moderate middle-class men who might otherwise have supported the Republic were disillusioned by the Versailles demands.

Germany's military tradition was retained, despite the failure of the war, and perpetuated in the Ebert-Groener pact with the army which elevated the military and increased its confidence. This survival of right-wing power was a major cause of the political troubles of the early 1920s. The Kapp Putsch, the Munich Putsch and the numerous assassinations, riots and troubles inspired by military forces such as the Freikorps and Stahelm all showed the power of right-wing military tradition. There were many factors at stake and it is understandable why there was so much political unrest in this period. However, it is probably fair to say that economic problems were the prime cause of instability, as in adverse economic circumstances, men have far less to lose by engaging in rebellion.

e This answer gives a full picture of the economic problems and links them throughout to the political troubles of the times. The knowledge is accurate and comprehensive, providing a clear and convincing response. The penultimate paragraph introduces some balance and there is a good coverage of other factors here. Finally, the conclusion prioritises between factors and not only makes it clear that one is deemed more important than others, but also explains why. This is a high-quality answer that would merit 15/15 marks.

paper 2

Time allowed: 1 hour 30 minutes.

You are advised to spend about 45 minutes on each question.

Answer Question 1 and **either** Question 2 **or** Question 3.

Question 1 Germany, 1914–25

Source A: *Adapted from an account of the Versailles Settlement written in 1923 by the lawyer chiefly responsible for the Weimar Constitution of 1919, Hugo Preuss*

The German Republic was born out of terrible defeat. This cast from the first a dark shadow on the new political order. The criminal madness of the Versailles Diktat was a shameless blow in the face (to hopes of political and economic recovery). The Weimar Constitution was born with this curse upon it. That it did not collapse immediately under the strain is striking proof of the genuine vitality of its basic principles, but its development was fatefully restricted thereby.

Source B:

A poster captioned 'Clemenceau the Vampire', from the conservative German newspaper, Kladderadatsch, July 1919

Source C: From The German Question and Europe *by P. Alter, 2000*

The Germans failed to appreciate the moderating influence exerted by the British on the Allies' deliberations, when they began in Paris in January 1919. Bearing in mind that Germany had willingly started the war and that, during the war, both sides in the conflict had voiced far-reaching plans for annexations, the Versailles Peace Treaty was, in fact, quite moderate. This is often overlooked in the face of the noisy complaints and condemnations made by its critics in later years. All the propaganda against the Treaty was highly exaggerated. The Germans probably did not fully grasp how lightly they had escaped the consequences of war and defeat.

(a) **Study Source A. Using your own knowledge, explain briefly what is meant by the term 'Versailles Diktat' in the context of 1919.** (3 marks)

(b) **Study Sources B and C. With reference to your own knowledge, explain how the view expressed in Source C challenges the view of the Versailles Peace Treaty put forward by the cartoonist in Source B.** (7 marks)

(c) **Study Sources A, B, and C and use your own knowledge. In what ways was the Treaty of Versailles a disaster for the Weimar Republic? Explain your answer with reference to the period 1919–25.** (15 marks)

Total: 25 marks

■ ■ ■

How to tackle paper 2, question 1(a)

A basic definition, which might earn 1 mark, would explain 'Diktat' as something that was imposed, not negotiated. For full marks this would have to be explained further and set in context. Something might, for example, be said about the Treaty of Versailles. Reference to issues such as Germany being stripped of land and colonies, its army being reduced in size, being forced to accept the war guilt clause, being made to pay reparations would all help explain the Diktat. Even better would be a comment on the German reaction to the Treaty; why the Germans regarded this as a 'Diktat' and how there were those who felt under little moral obligation to honour it.

The danger to avoid here is a long explanation of the terms of the Versailles Treaty. The greater the concentration on the word 'Diktat', the better. Remember that although you should refer to the source, you will not gain marks for merely repeating what the source says, so always try to provide some relevant 'own knowledge' in this type of question.

How to tackle paper 2, question 1(b)

You need to observe the different views of the Peace Treaty put forward in these two sources. A common fault is to list what one source says and then the other — in this case describing the poster. It is better to jot down points first and then write a comparative answer. For example, you might note the following:

Source B
- Clemenceau (France) is sucking the lifeblood of Germany.
- Germany (the woman) has laid down arms but can do nothing — she is at the mercy of the French.

Source C
- The Treaty was quite moderate.
- The Germans escaped lightly.

Do not miss the point in Source C that speaks of the 'moderating influence of the British'. This could be held to support Source B, which only shows the French (not the British) as vampires. You need to refer to your own knowledge. Do not make the mistake of concentrating on the sources alone; this will limit your mark to 2/7. For the highest marks, you should comment on the attitudes of the various parties at Versailles and draw conclusions as to which source is more convincing and why these sources differ. The obvious point to make here is that Source B is a clear piece of German political propaganda from a contemporary, conservative newspaper (make use of the information given in the title), whereas Source C is the view of a modern historian trying to question assumptions.

How to tackle paper 2, question 1(c)

You will probably have plenty of information on the Treaty of Versailles, but the important thing to remember is that you need to use your information to answer the question, not merely present it as a narrative. A short essay plan might help you formulate your ideas before you begin writing. The plan below is longer than the one you would write, but it is provided to give you some guidelines.

The following steps should ensure a good answer:
- Consider (a) which terms of the Treaty created problems for the Republic and (b) what those problems were.
- Ask yourself whether the Treaty was a complete disaster. (Remember that you should always try to include some alternative viewpoints to get a balanced answer.)
- Do not forget to refer to the sources. If you only write from your own knowledge you cannot score more than 8/15 marks.
- Have some idea of what your conclusion will be before you begin. Try to make your view clear at the outset and ensure that you show some judgement.

Suggested plan

In what ways was the Treaty a disaster?

(a) Which terms created problems? (Refer to Source B)
- Damaging: loss of territory, especially economically valuable areas such as the Saar Basin, Alsace-Lorraine, part of Silesia and all the colonies. The imposition of reparations.

- Humiliating: the demilitarisation and 15-year occupation of the Rhineland, the Polish Corridor dividing German territory, the clause forbidding Anschluss (union) with Austria, the reduction of the German army and navy and the forced acceptance of war guilt. (Source A: 'this curse'; Source B: 'humiliated and drained')

(b) What were the problems? (Refer to Source A)
- The Treaty harmed democracy — its terms provided fuel for the extremists who branded the Weimar politicians as 'November Criminals'. Not only extremists but also moderates, who might otherwise have supported the Republic, turned against it.
- The Treaty exacerbated Germany's postwar economic difficulties and laid burdens of reparations that it could not cope with. Reparations helped cause the hyper-inflation of 1923.
- The military was angered and determined to reassert its strength. The disarmament issue precipitated the Kapp Putsch of 1920.
- The Treaty exacerbated problems already inherent in Germany — particularly social and economic divisions.

In what ways was the Treaty not a disaster? (Refer to Source C)
- The breakup of the Austro-Hungarian, Russian and Turkish empires meant that Germany was now surrounded by small weak states which might provide opportunities for future change.
- Germany was not permanently weakened. It still had plentiful economic resources, the nucleus of an army and most of its territory in Europe. (Source C: limited annexations)
- Source A refers to the resilience and 'vitality' of the Republic. The basic institutions were unscathed, at least until 1925.
- Reparations were not so burdensome that they destroyed the German economy. They were probably more harmful psychologically than economically. The hyper-inflation of 1923 was the result of the French occupation of the Ruhr, not of reparations in themselves, and Stresemann negotiated their reorganisation through the Dawes Plan of 1924.

Conclusion
It might be fair to conclude that while the Treaty did not help the birth of the Weimar Republic, by the mid-1920s it was not causing much actual damage. The only problem was that when things did go wrong, for example in the crisis of 1923, it provided fuel for the extremist politicians such as Hitler. Source C points out that propaganda (like Source B) exaggerated the problems. Maybe 'disaster' is too strong a word?

Question 2 Germany, 1871–90

Read the following source and then answer the questions which follow:

In 1890 Bismarck could look back with some satisfaction on his achievements. He had united the German Empire, yet preserved Prussian conservative influence, scored victory over his opponents and ensured that Germany held a respected and dominant role in Europe.

(a) **What is meant by Prussian conservative influence in the context of the German Empire from 1871?**   (3 marks)

(b) **Explain the ways in which Bismarck scored victory over his opponents during his time as Chancellor.**   (7 marks)

(c) **Do you agree that Germany in 1890 had more strengths than weaknesses? Explain your answer.**   (15 marks)

Total: 25 marks

■ ■ ■

How to tackle paper 2, question 2(a)

The key words of the question (which it is often helpful to underline) are 'Prussia', 'conservative' and '1871'. You might refer to the following:

- Prussia's dominance in the unification process, which was Prussian aggrandisement.
- Conservatism as a political doctrine that favours keeping things as they are, with power in the hands of the traditional monarchy supported by the upper classes (as opposed to liberal ideas of representative government).
- The hostility of Prussia's kings to liberal ideas and the power of Prussia's feudal landowning class, the Junkers.
- The Prussian-dominated constitution in the new German empire of 1871. Prussia provided the King and the Chancellor and dominated the Bundesrat (the upper house of Parliament), where it effectively had a veto.

Make it clear that you have understood what 'Prussian conservative influence' means, both in general terms and in the context of the new German empire.

How to tackle paper 2, question 2(b)

The obvious line here is to look at Bismarck's victory over the Catholics in the Kulturkampf and over the socialists from 1878. These represent only two opponents, however, and an answer that only covered these areas could be rather narrow.

Try to reflect on the wider implications of the question. How could you use other information here? Consider the following:

- Bismarck's victory over the liberals in creating a constitution which 'preserved Prussian conservative influence'. This was a mark of his personal skill and standing and his support from the Kaiser.
- Bismarck's victory over Kaiser Wilhelm I in disputes, achieved by threats of resignation.
- Bismarck's victory over the Reichstag — particularly over the army budget — achieved by the use of political manoeuvres, alliances, dissolution and election to win majority support (e.g. playing on the scare of war with France, 1875 and 1887).
- Bismarck's victory over the National Liberals, particularly after 1878 when the party divided after the Protection Crisis (a small number followed Bismarck, the rest split into various splinter groups), caused by shifting alliances.
- Bismarck's victory over the Centre Party, both in the Kulturkampf and in the 1880s, when he played on war scares to create the 1887 Kartell of Conservatives and National Liberals.

Notice that the way in which Bismarck scored his victory is explained in each case. The question is less concerned with *where* he was victorious than *why*: an important distinction.

Finally, do not forget that you will need to prioritise the factors. Consider which were Bismarck's most important, or most complete, victories and show links between them (e.g. the victory over the various political parties is an aspect of Bismarck's victory over the Reichstag). You will need to draw conclusions. Try to question Bismarck's 'victory', which might be used in inverted commas to show that the term is not altogether appropriate, and consider whether Bismarck's campaigns against the Catholics, Centre Party, socialists and so on really succeeded. Did he ever have complete victory over the Reichstag? Surely he never really scored victory over the Kaiser, particularly in view of what happened in 1890.

How to tackle paper 2, question 2(c)

You should already have a plan for this answer if you have gone through the table of the strengths and weaknesses of Germany in 1890 given in the Content Guidance section (p. 16), so it should be comparatively simple to put your points together in a convincing essay.

Remember that you need:

- a paragraph structure (make a short plan first)
- an argument — are you going to agree or disagree with the question? This is likely to affect the way you order your material
- a conclusion that makes clear which side you are on and why, and what the most important strength/weakness was and why

Try writing your own response, and then compare it with the following answer.

By the time of the fall of Bismarck in 1890 Germany had many strengths. It had been a united country for 20 years and had a written constitution. This included the Bundesrat and the Reichstag, which was elected every 5 years by manhood suffrage with a secret ballot. The Kaiser was at the head of the government and appointed the Chancellor. Bismarck worked well with Kaiser Wilhelm I and together they created a stable state. By 1890 Bismarck had defeated most of his enemies in the Reichstag. He had carried out the Kulturkampf against the Catholics, weakened the liberals and although he had not destroyed the socialists, his anti-socialist laws had undermined them.

Unification had helped make Germany strong. Industry was growing and the output of basic materials like coal, iron and steel had increased since 1870. The new electrical and chemical industries were doing well. Agriculture benefited from the use of fertilisers and modern equipment. Germany was also strong militarily. It had been unified by war, and the traditions of the powerful Prussian army made Germany a strong power that was feared and respected by other nations.

There were weaknesses, however. Prussia had led unification, and the new German Emperor was also the King of Prussia. Prussia held the largest number of seats in the Bundesrat and could veto any legislation it did not like. This led to a feeling that Prussia had 'conquered' the rest of Germany, and some Germans, particularly those in the south, resented this. Some German peoples, such as the Austrians, were still excluded from the new Germany, while other 'foreigners', such as Poles, French and Danes, were included in the empire.

The constitution was full of weaknesses. The Kaiser still had considerable powers and chose his own ministers and chancellor. When the Reichstag proved awkward, the Chancellor could ask the Kaiser to dissolve it. The Bundesrat, dominated by Prussia, could also block laws of which it disapproved, so there was therefore little opportunity for the ordinary people to influence decisions. The Chancellor himself was actually in a weak position, as he was totally dependent on the Kaiser. This became clear when Wilhelm II became Kaiser and decided to get rid of Bismarck. The rights of the individual German states were also a weakness in the constitution because they could control matters such as law and order. Some even had their own armies and the different states collected their own taxes.

Bismarck's policies had also helped to weaken Germany. His methods of controlling the Reichstag, and in particular the way he dissolved it when he faced opposition, weakened parliamentary government. His attack on the Centre Party, National Liberals and SPD weakened party politics, and the socialists were left feeling particularly bitter. Even the economic growth of

Germany was a weakness in some respects, as it created industrial problems of housing and working conditions. It also made the working classes a more powerful group in society, and yet they were unable to influence politics through the Socialist Party. Finally, Germany's powerful military reputation could be seen as a weakness as it encouraged worldwide ambitions, although this was not a particular problem in 1890.

It is therefore inaccurate to say that Germany had more strengths than weaknesses. Although Germany did have a number of strengths, it had more weaknesses. It has been described as 'a political dwarf but an economic giant', and this sums up its position very effectively. When Bismarck fell from power he left a country that was economically and socially one of the most modern and dynamic in Europe, but since he had concentrated power in his own hands he had obstructed the growth of representative government in Germany. The weaknesses in the Imperial Constitution which prevented the Reichstag having a greater influence in government were without doubt the greatest hindrance to the future development of Germany. It was unfortunate that in 1890 government fell into the hands of a Kaiser whose traditionalism and irresponsibility curbed the political development of Germany still further.

Comment on this essay

How did you do? If you produced something similar to the answer given here, well done. This is a grade A answer. It is not particularly sophisticated, but it covers a good range of points in a clear and logical manner, and brings them together in an effective conclusion.

Question 3 Germany, 1890–1914

Look at the following statistics showing the structure of the German labour force (in thousands) and then answer the questions which follow:

Occupation	1895	1913
Agriculture	9,788	10,701
Mining	432	863
Manufacturing	7,524	10,857
Transport	620	1,174
Commerce	1,970	3,474
Domestic service	1,571	1,542

(a) **How might these statistics increase our understanding of changes in the German economy 1895–1913?** (3 marks)

(b) **Explain why the German economy developed so rapidly after 1895.** (7 marks)

(c) **'The social results of economic change caused more problems for the rulers of Germany than any other issue.' Explain why you agree or disagree with this statement with reference to German domestic history 1890–1914.** (15 marks)

Total: 25 marks

■ ■ ■

How to tackle paper 2, question 3(a)

This question adopts a slightly different approach to the other 'part (a)' questions on these two examination papers. You are required to extract relevant information from statistics and *show how this increases our understanding* of changes in the German economy. Do not waste time trying to work out percentages or doing complicated sums. Remember that this is just a 3-mark question and the examiner is only expecting you to comment on overall patterns.

The obvious point to make is the huge growth in industrial employment (mining, manufacturing, transport and commerce) compared to the minimal growth in agriculture and the decline in domestic service. From these statistics we learn that:

- the German economy was developing along modern, industrial lines
- the development of the economy was accompanied by social change, which had reduced the numbers entering domestic service
- agriculture was (comparatively) in decline
- the changes had taken place rapidly

You must show some of your own knowledge in your answer, perhaps pointing out that there was a huge acceleration in the output of heavy industry after 1890 (coal, iron and steel), stimulated in part by the continued growth of the railway system and the development of the German navy (transport). You could also mention the growth of the new electrical and chemical manufacturing industries. The decline of agriculture was a result of the competition faced from cheap American imports of grain carried to Germany in vast steamships.

You do not need to include all this information. As long as you have shown that you understand the statistics and can explain them using your own knowledge, you will score well.

How to tackle paper 2, question 3(b)

You need to present a range of factors here, so try to include as many points as you can — making links, and prioritising between factors. Here are some suggestions:

- Foundations laid under Bismarck: unification provided resources, for example iron ore from Alsace-Lorraine. Beneficial legislation laid the foundations for economic growth; for example, the removal of internal tariffs, uniform currency, standard commercial law and the formation of the Reichsbank.

- Geographical factors: central position of the country, flat land in the north for railways, rivers, resources, coal, iron and chemical deposits.
- A large and expanding population (providing labour force and consumers).
- Expansion of educational facilities (especially scientific and technical education).
- New industrial inventions and techniques, e.g. Siemens (the electric dynamo in 1867, electronic traction after 1879).
- Stimulus in development of new products, electrical goods, chemicals and the motor car.
- Stimulus through growth in railways and shipping.
- Sophisticated banking system: free of state control and providing easy credit.
- Commercial organisation favouring large combines (cartels), e.g. Siemens/Halske and AEG (German Electrical Company). By 1903 the Westphalian Coal Syndicate controlled half Germany's coal production. By 1905 there were 306 cartels.
- Government support, e.g. trade treaties with Italy, Austria, Russia, Belgium etc. in the 1890s — this reduced duties on agricultural products coming into Germany, which hit farmers, but in return gained markets for German manufactured goods.

You will need to present your ideas in a coherent way and should try to stress the most important factors, e.g. the effect of the expanding population coupled with the government-backed opportunities provided by the educational, banking and organisational systems. It does not really matter what you emphasise, as long as you can make a reasonable case.

How to tackle paper 2, question 3(c)

The danger here is to launch into an account of the plight of the working classes and the history of the SPD without thinking this question through. Instead, break the question down.

Stop to consider what the social results of economic change were.
- The creation of an élite of powerful industrialists anxious to preserve their status and wealth.
- The expansion of the middle class, comprising businessmen, bankers, manufacturers, people with trading interests, insurance brokers etc.
- Urbanisation.
- A huge expansion in the industrial working class.
- A decline in the position of the landowners and the numbers of those dependent on agriculture.

Next, think about the problems they caused for the government.
- The conservatism of the industrial élites (who wanted to protect what they had gained) and the entrenched conservatism of the Junker landowners (as they fought to preserve their status and influence in the face of economic change) were

powerful forces shaping government. But this influence was challenged by the liberals and socialists.

- The liberalism of the middle classes (but remember they were unable to exert much influence on policies — their outcry over 'civil rights' in the Zabern Affair of 1913 had no effect on the Kaiser).
- The solidarity, organisation and political awareness of the working class, which increased as urbanisation brought members more closely together. Those anxious to improve living and working conditions and provide for a better future for their offspring were attracted by trade unionism and socialism.

Analyse the problems, and see how great they were.

- The élites were alarmed by the growing strength of the Socialist Party (SPD). Give some statistics, e.g. in 1893 the socialists won the most votes, in 1912 the most seats.
- The socialists' intentions were not entirely clear. They were committed to measures to help the working classes, and at the Erfurt Conference in 1891 they officially adopted the Marxist (revolutionary) line with its ideas of a classless society. However, many socialists were quite prepared to work within the Reichstag, respected the monarchy and supported imperial foreign policy. These 'revisionists' had no desire to provoke a revolution, but the measures taken against them weakened this moderate element and encouraged clashes with the right.
- The Centre Party held the balance between right and left. The government was forced to adopt policies to please this group and deflect them from association with the socialists, whose social and economic demands seemed more threatening to the élites.
- This right-wing/left-wing polarisation (landowners and industrialists who refused to give up any of their power and wealth in contrast with the workers who were demanding greater rights) undermined the German parliamentary system and showed the weakness of the Reichstag. It may even have encouraged Germany's aggressive foreign policy to whip up the patriotic support of the middle classes and deflect attention away from problems at home.

Refer to your knowledge of how these clashes troubled the politics of the Wilhelmine era.

- Caprivi's free-trade measures (1890s) reflected the waning influence of the Junkers. They fought back through the Agrarian League.
- After Caprivi's fall (1894) the Kaiser's attitude helped polarise the two sides. His attempts to combat the growing threat from the socialists led to clashes with the Reichstag (1894–99), which forced the dropping of anti-socialist and anti-unionist legislation.
- *Sammlungspolitik* (1897) attempted to harness conservative interests in the Reich and bridge the gap between Junker and industrialist. The success of the Agrarian League and the reimposition of tariffs (1902) were a sign of the government moving back to old-fashioned conservatism. Big business was appeased by the growth of the navy and *Weltpolitik*, putting the emphasis on foreign policy.

- After 1912 the socialists destroyed Bülow's bloc of parties and were in a position to resist any unpopular government legislation. Although the Zabern incident (1913) showed Wilhelm II acting high-handedly and the weakness of the Reichstag, the furore over this shows how massive anti-government feeling could be mobilised.

Finally, examine whether these problems were greater than any other issue. Try to think of a variety of other problems, e.g. military dominance, the primacy of foreign and imperial policy, the faults of the constitution, the inefficacy of the Kaiser's chancellors. Show which you regard as the most important — and make sure you explain why and support your reasoning. This should lead to a brief conclusion in which you try to summarise the problems, stressing the most important, and make it clear whether you agree or disagree with the statement.